Moving to the Dominican Republic:

The Paradox of Paradise

by

Ross Weber

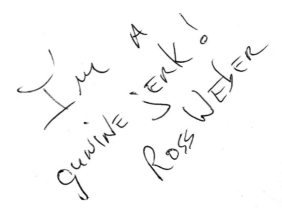

I'm a genuine jerk!
Ross Weber

To the most beautiful woman in the world:
my wife.
Thank you for making me feel
lucky every day!

Table of Contents

Introduction

"In the end, it is not the years in your life that count.
It is the life in your years."

Abraham Lincoln

Living life to its fullest is just the way I do things.

Sometimes the way I do things causes me severe consequences. At other times, my curiosity requires me to be patient, tardy, or humble enough to admit I messed up. There have, however, not been many times when life has not been exciting. Life is great; at least, that's what I tell myself every day when I wake up. Now, I consider myself young, but I am definitely not a kid. Due to the variety of experiences I have had in my life, I consider myself fairly easygoing and well versed in dealing with different lifestyles and people.

I have been to four of the seven continents. I have visited countries spanning the globe from North to South, and from West to East. During my travels, I have had the opportunity to meet and get to know many diverse groups of people. I have done business with Eskimos in Alaska and Indian natives in Canada. I have shared views and perspectives with Aborigines in Australia. I have been fishing, hunting, and game-spotting with natives in several African countries. I have friends who live on every continent, probably in just about every country.

I am an avid outdoorsman who loves the wild and

enjoys exploring new destinations. I have climbed some of the highest peaks in the United States. I have been to the lowest points on both the African and North American continents. I have climbed the tallest sand dunes in the world. I have been in the bush in Australia, the jungles of Central America, and the tropics of Malaysia. I have been deep-sea fishing in the Pacific, the Atlantic, and the Caribbean. I have also lived in climates ranging from 120+ to -30. Throughout my life I have many incredible memories.

Some of my most memorable experiences include feeling the true textures of an alligator's skin and the hair of an elephant; tasting the flesh of a shark; hunting a species of antelope which at one time was on the endangered species list; hearing the breath of a lion outside my tent at night; smelling the odor of a giant elk as it walked past me; and petting a cheetah while it purred like a motor. These experiences, among others, have often made me feel as if I had been everywhere and done everything: but that was before I visited the Dominican Republic for the first time.

The Dominican Republic is a country with a million unique smells and a multitude of new sights and sounds. From the songbirds to the *motos* and music, the Dominican Republic has a natural noise of its own. The smells of the ocean air, fresh fruits, and Dominican cuisine contrast sharply with the heavy stench of exhaust from the thousands of vehicles. On top of the new smells and sounds, the country is literally alive with color. The locals are proud of their buildings and make sure you know it by painting them all sorts of bright colors.

Like the locals, the island itself is proud, because its soil grows some of the most colorful vegetation I have ever seen. The bushes, plants, trees, and vines grow naturally in every shade of the rainbow, yet there are places with no color at all. The island has well over a thousand different shades of orange, green, and yellow, but rust, brown and grey thrive equally as well. Hundreds of different species of birds sport almost every color imaginable. There are birds with red plumage; there are birds with blue plumage. There are even ordinary everyday pigeons. The country also supports many exotic species of parrots and finches, which sing and whistle almost to the point of insanity.

The island is tropical, which allows it to boast some of the most beautiful landscapes imaginable. It is home to a very diverse population, among whom live some of the most impoverished people on the planet. On any given day, it is not uncommon to see a person driving a Ferrari – but you will surely see another riding a cart drawn by a horse. The locals can live in a building the size of a shopping center, but they are also comfortable living under a tarp.

This is a country that owes much of its current oppression to a tyrannical dictator, a short-sighted man who raped the country of its most prized possessions. He took from both rich and poor. He lived the life of a king, while depriving the people of happiness and advancement by restricting access to schools, medicine, and technology. Due directly to this dictator's stranglehold on the country, at one point a majority of the Dominican population was unable to read.

The modern-day Dominican Republic has a democratically-elected government, with a President, Congress, and a functioning court system. The country is known for its vast production of sugar and coffee, as well as its abundance of other natural resources like amber. It is popular with tourists for its variety of beautiful virgin beaches, which range from pure white to almost black. It produces wonderful baseball players who dominate the major leagues, as well as beautiful women who are the envy of exotic fashion. Very widely known is its incredible *merengue* music, which, like most folk music, tells the stories of the people and different events in their lives. It is a country truly different from any other on the planet.

As you get to know the Dominican Republic, you will quickly notice the friendliness of the people. They will give you a good meal and an even better conversation. They will invite you to their house for the weekend, and in return, expect you to talk with them. Dominicans are amazing, just like the island that has raised them. Yet the Dominican people are as diverse as the islands' birds, plants, and beaches. They can be tall or short, dark or pale. The only similarity between any two Dominicans is their insuperable love for their heritage. Who would blame them? Their country is beautiful and their culture is strong. They are Dominicans, and they live by their own set of rules.

Dominicans live in a country where many North American, European, or *gringo* cultures and traditions simply do not apply. They live on a tropical island that is being forced to enter the modern era at the speed of technology, while still having the infrastructure of the past century. These differences are unique in that the people know what is modern, yet many of their lifestyles and habits are outdated. Lifestyle differences and habits are the cause of major cultural differences between the DR and the first world. Disparities are magnified because the island is a vacation getaway for many wealthy foreigners who demand first-world amenities. This book will focus on these cultural differences and how to deal with them.

One of my first observations when I came to the island was that there is no such thing as a "true Dominican." You can't judge by a person's looks whether or not he's a Dominican. Dominicans are simply different, and they are proud of this. The country's population has influences from Europe, Africa, Asia, and of course many Latin influences. One of the representations of this national recognition of individuality is the ubiquitous doll without a face. As you enter the airport, take a quick look in the shops, look in your hotel's gift shop, and look at many stores around the country. You'll see these dolls everywhere.

The doll without a face is designed to represent all Dominicans, because it allows its viewers to place the face as they wish, which is uniquely individual. The dolls are faceless to represent the wide number of possible faces that could fit on each doll. Remember that Dominicans appreciate being viewed as individuals. They are proud of their personal differences. The doll without a face is a symbol of a faceless people; each individual is unique. As you adapt to the Dominican Republic and its culture, remember your own personal uniqueness and individuality; but keep in mind that Dominicans also see themselves as similar to each other. They all eat plantains. They all like fried cheese and salami. They are proud of their *Mangu*. My intentions in this book are to help you adjust to the cultural differences and similarities as you begin your journey of becoming *aplatanado*.

I have divided this book into two parts. The first part has more to do with my own story. Why have I moved to the Dominican Republic? How was I able to make ends meet financially? What was the first level of lessons I learned as I made the transition? How did I deal with the culture shock and the differences in my new society? What were my safeguards? How did I approach certain situations that could have had bad outcomes? What were some of the hardest things for me to overcome as I left my family, my country, and my life in the United States? These are just a few of the questions I hope to answer in the first part of the book.

The second part will deal with more general questions: issues like safety, travel, resources, and preparing to make the move on your own. I believe the second part will be useful for you to look back on from time to time, and to use as a reference guide.

PART ONE

Living in a country so vastly different from any I have ever lived in has required both education and patience. Sometimes my ability to learn and remain calm has been tested by the country's backward approach to problems. One of my strategies for keeping the often backward-seeming approaches from driving me crazy is always to tell everyone "I love it here," and to remind myself that there are plenty of things to love.

What do I mean by that? Well, the Dominican Republic does have its major challenges. The electricity grid is terrible. The police are corrupt. Traffic is horrendous. And as for crime… well, let's just say you always need to be looking over your shoulder. Each of these areas presents a new challenge.

In addition, Dominican time runs a little slower than anywhere else I have ever lived. Added together, these challenges sometimes make me want to scream! With that said, I really do love the Dominican Republic. And I believe many Americans would be happier living here than they are in their current environment, particularly now with the world economic crisis and the rapidly-declining real estate values. I always tell everyone I love it here, because no matter whether some small thing is driving me nuts at the moment or not, I really do love this country. It is an amazing place.

There's Plenty to Love about the DR

If one were to make a list of items to treasure about the Dominican Republic, the list would be very long.

Items on my own list include my ability to go running outdoors every day of the year. And then there are the wonderful fruit and vegetables I find for sale on every corner. I have never eaten so many avocados, mangos, papayas, *limoncillos*, guavas, bananas, and other fruits never even imagined in the United States. I make it a point to have some sort of fresh fruit in my house all the time. If I ever run low, it's easy to walk to the corner vendor and buy more. The corner vendors sell fruit from makeshift carts that are part bicycle, part umbrella. They pile the fruit so high the mounds amount to more than one could carry in two wheelbarrows. These heaps of fresh fruit are so colorful they tempt the eye almost as much as they tempt the tongue. You cannot get within ten feet of the street vendors' carts without smelling the sweet honey-like aroma of the ripe fruits. Even thinking about the smell of the fresh pineapple, papaya, bananas, or mangos sitting in the warm air makes my mouth water. I have also learned to love sour oranges, which replace salad dressing and are a delight.

Another one of the beauties of living in a developing country, and something I will surely mention many times throughout this book, is the fact that I now have a housekeeper and cook. I absolutely love it! The fact that I can have someone come to my house and cook and clean, even though I am just a normal dude, is great!

Having a housekeeper and cook is one of the things I would never trade, because one of my least favorite tasks is washing dirty dishes. The seemingly simple ability just to have someone there to do the cooking and cleaning is something so wonderful I cannot explain it. My whole life, I have washed my dirty clothes once or twice a week. I have always washed my dishes every day, but still there always seemed to be a growing pile waiting to be cleaned. It is so unbelievably cool not to have to wash laundry (I haven't washed a load of laundry in almost four years!), not to have to wash dishes, and to have someone cook what you want and then ask if you would like coffee or dessert afterwards. I would have never realized how much I appreciate having household help if I had not been more or less forced into hiring someone. At first it was a little weird for me to tell someone to make me lunch. However, for Dominicans of every class, household help is just a normal part of life. It is a luxury that ordinary citizens of first-world countries miss out on.

Another thing I absolutely love about the Dominican Republic is the strength of good Dominican families. It is astonishing to me to see families where the children are grown up, have families of their own, and yet they still help their brothers and sisters out. Most adult children visit their parents on the weekends so they can sit and talk. As parents become older, the children view it as their duty to have their parents move in with their family so they can repay them for the care they were given as a child. This kind of treatment or bond just does not seem to exist much in the United States.

Even though I am not a member of the Catholic church (by far the most widely-practiced religion on the island), I also love the fact that it is quite normal for someone to say a prayer at the beginning of most public events. One event I remember in particular was a race I entered on the *Mirador* one weekend. Just before the race began, they prayed as a group. There were several hundred people standing there in a public park while the MC prayed that everyone would be healthy and run a good race. It almost made me fall over, I was so shocked.

I have also taken dance classes at a local dance school. The school has a prayer at the end of class each day. It is no big deal; you are not forced to join them. They simply offer a prayer before people go their separate ways. They pray that you will be safe and that God will help you learn as you practice. It is a simple thing, but something many living in modernized first-world countries would not even think of. Whether you are religious or not, in my opinion it is awesome to see people so humble and grateful for what they have been given. I respect that humility.

As you read this book, you will soon learn that I also love the many other treasures this beautiful country has. As I explain the cultural differences, I will discuss times I have had difficulties adjusting, and areas where I could have planned my transition better. Hopefully, these examples will help you learn how to steer clear of similar problems. I hope you decide to join me sometime. Living in the Dominican Republic is AWESOME!

Now, let me tell you a little about my background and how I came to know the Dominican Republic.

A Little Bit about Me

First of all, I am only including this section so you know enough about me to understand I am just a normal dude who was raised in a normal American family. Prior to coming to the DR I had NO Spanish skills. I could not even speak one sentence in Spanish. I am a short bald white guy, who was raised in a middle class American family. My family had nothing special with regard to income or lifestyle; the latter was even more restricted which was compounded because my parents are severely conservative.

I had never been to the Caribbean and did not think of myself as much of a risk- taker prior to my first visit. When I decided to move, I was 31 years old and single. I had just under $150,000 in debt from student loans and was just beginning my professional life. When I had the opportunity to visit the first time, I realized that I could either go or not go. Short-term, the one-week vacation would not really affect me professionally. Either way, five years down the road, it would be a one-week trip I would remember well.

What I did not know at the time was that short-term, one-week vacation would change my life.

After my first trip to the Dominican Republic, I started to look at things differently with regard to my life and what I wanted to accomplish. I began to justify why it was good for me to continue to visit. I started by scheduling a second visit a few weeks later. After the second visit, it made sense to visit twice a month, at least for a year. These small justifications started out as ways for me to be able to return more quickly than most tourists, but ultimately, they were the reasons why I ended up eventually moving. In order to feel another visit was a good idea, I would tell myself, "If I visited again, things could go well and change my life for the better. If things went badly, I would have had a great year, and I could start fresh again a year older." What the heck? You only live once. With my constantly-advancing justifications, I continued to visit and stretch my comfort level with living abroad. I also was learning about how to maintain my job and contacts while frequently being out of the country.

My Experience with Education

Before we move much further, let me take a step back in time and tell you a little about my childhood. I was born and raised in a small town in Southern California. I lived there until I was sixteen years old. When I was sixteen, I felt I was grown up enough to live on my own; so I decided it was time to move out of my parents' house. I also wanted to be away from the watchful eyes of my parents. My solution was to move about 1000 miles away and live with some friends who were going to college in Utah.

I stayed in Utah until I was about twenty-six years old. While I lived in Utah, I worked at several health clubs and became very good at selling health club memberships. I ran a promotions team that went door-to-door, selling memberships to college students. We also sold memberships through promotions at the local colleges and malls. Looking back on the many years I have spent in school and the variety of jobs I have worked since I moved out of my parents' home, it is probably the health club sales training that has had the greatest impact on my life. Learning to sell and use sales strategies effectively has been one of the most important lessons I have learned.

After graduating from college with a Bachelor's degree (at age twenty-six), I moved to Moscow, Idaho to attend law school and to obtain an MBA. I chose the school in Moscow because it has a concurrent enrollment JD/MBA with a sister school a few miles away. Moscow is a tiny town in the far northern panhandle of Idaho. I spent the next three years reading, reading, and reading. It was cold, wet, and basically just miserable in Moscow.

I learned to read continually for hours on end. Over the three years, I went from having 20/20 vision to needing glasses to be able to function.

As a JD/MBA student, I relied on student loans to survive, and I lived on a very low budget. I had a small amount of money saved and did not want to go way into debt, so I moved into a trailer park to live as inexpensively as possible. My living conditions in Moscow were some of the poorest I have ever experienced in my life. Little did I know that the training on low-income living I was receiving would actually end up helping me deal with life in the Dominican Republic, without the normal luxuries.

I learned how to live with low electricity consumption, how to function without consistent running water, and how to eat just about any inexpensive food to survive. My tight budget constrained even the slightest splurging. Other than those few important lessons, nothing really significant enough to mention in this book happened in Moscow.

As graduation from law school approached, I was unable to find the right legal job to meet my ever growing need for a real paycheck. Before I began my education, I had been making about $40,000 a year selling health club memberships. I was not about to take a job as an attorney making the same or less, after seven years of studying and spending my weekends in the library. Since I couldn't find the right legal job, I decided to do what people with too much education often do: I decided to go to law school for another year.

While I was making up my mind about what to do next, I talked with friends, family and professors about my situation and what direction would best fit my future. One of my professors recommended I go to Harvard or

American University, because these two schools had great
international programs. I discovered it would take me a year
to get into Harvard, so I applied to American University. I
was accepted within a week and moved to Washington, DC
about two weeks later.

I had been accepted at one of the top International
Trade Law schools in the world. The majority of the
students in the program were foreigners, with only five
or six Americans. I was both excited and a little nervous
about this change. I was moving from a tiny town with
but a handful of traffic lights to the capital of the most
powerful country in the world. I had no idea that this year
in DC would be a turning point in my life. In the end, I
made my decision to go to school in DC very quickly. I
was at a point where I would either have to leave Moscow
immediately to start classes, or I would have to wait for
another nine months to be able to enroll. Although I had
been working hard to find the right job, I believed I would
have better opportunities if I did a year's specialization.
Now that I think about it, things happened really fast.
Maybe even way too fast!

Culture Shock in the District of Columbia

The move from Northern Idaho to Washington, DC
was the second biggest culture shock I have experienced
in my life. I went from a town with three traffic lights to
the most powerful city in the world. I was literally lost in
the city. I was scared of the metro and had no clue how
to get around.

When you move to a new city in Idaho, you learn
your way around the city by getting in your truck and
driving around a little bit. In thirty minutes or so, you'll

almost always see something you recognize; and after a week you know the whole place. I tried this strategy out in DC and spent two entire nights completely lost. When I had driven around for several hours and realized I had no clue where I was, I looked for a freeway entrance. Once I located an entrance, I got on the freeway and began to drive. I drove until I saw an exit with a gas station. I left the freeway and stopped at the gas station, where I bought a map and got the attendant to show me the way back to the city.

I spent a year in Washington, DC; and – other than my immediate neighborhood – I never was able to find my way around the city very well. After a couple of months, I began using the Metro to go out with friends and to get around the city. Part of me thinks it is the fault of the Metro that I never conquered the streets of DC. In the spring, I learned the streets in my neighborhood quite well because I started to run. I ran every day for an hour or so, and I made it a point never to go the same way twice. Soon enough, I was able to get around my running area quite well.

(Later on, when I moved to the Dominican Republic, I used the same technique as I began to explore the Dominican capital, Santo Domingo. I would leave each morning for a run, never taking the same route. I would use some streets as markers and eventually ventured further and further around the city. I now know the city as well as people who have lived here most of their lives.)

While I was in DC, I tried to do all the sightseeing and tourist things, because I figured I wouldn't be living there forever. I also made it a point to do all these activities with the foreign students, rather than spending my free time with other Americans. I learned more about the world that year than I ever even dreamed. An event I will remember forever was an Ambassador's reception that took place the beginning of the second semester. The reception was given for students in the international program, and was attended by Ambassadors of many of the countries with students in the program. The whole night was wonderful – and at that reception, I would meet a person who would later change my life.

The entire first semester, my Dominican friend Julio had bragged about how awesome his country was. He told me about the beautiful beaches. He spoke of the amazing food. He was so enthusiastic about the country I figured he must be making it all up for my benefit. He was very excited that night at the reception, because I was going to meet one of his best friends from home. To this day, I blame Julio for my current living conditions in the DR. You see, he is the one who got the hottest girl I've ever met to attend American University.

Almost immediately after I met "Ana", I said to him, "Julio…Dude… if all the girls in your country look like her, I'm going to move there someday." At the time, he laughed and told people how funny the comment was. When I married Ana in La Vega, Dominican Republic in December 2007, Julio was a guest of honor.

Now, keep in mind that although I'm trained as a lawyer, I have never worked in a law firm, not for one day. I have always worked for corporations, often as a consultant. I pride myself on my people skills, which enable me to excel in areas like marketing, promotions, and sales. I work well with people and have the ability to adapt, which is how I was able to move to the DR and fit right in. One of the reasons I have done so well is my ability to get along with people from all walks of life. I always remember a statement my dad constantly used when I was a child. He would say: "Hey, boy – remember, everyone puts their pants on one leg at a time." He meant we are all the same, no matter where we were raised. It doesn't matter what we look like; it doesn't matter what we were given by our parents. We are all the same. No, my dad's not Dominican; but yes, he does have a doll without a face.

DC to the DR – the Beginning of My Odyssey

Graduation from American University didn't change my luck at all with regard to finding the right legal job. I had taken every dime in student loans just to live over the past year, but the job offers I was receiving were not even close to what I was worth. For example, I was offered a temp job in DC for $50,000 a year. The problem was, it would have cost me around $30,000 just to live, and the job was not guaranteed after the initial six-month contract. The unknown really scared me. I could probably have gotten legal jobs in California, Utah or Idaho, but lawyers in Utah and Idaho live just barely above poverty, in my opinion. And considering the number of hours they put in, they are surviving below the poverty level.

I sent out close to 3000 resumes to top law firms around the world and got nothing but unacceptable offers and a bunch of junk mail in return. Suddenly, one day it hit me: "What are you doing? You know how to sell! Why not work for a company who will pay you to help them sell something?" So that's what I did. I started working with a company that sold web marketing training, software and hosting services. When I started I felt like it wasn't the position I had gone to school for nine years to get, but they paid me really well.

When I started working with the company, I was living in a small room in my parents' basement in Utah because I had not determined where I would settle down. I was just going to stay there for a short time until I paid off some of the bills I had accumulated the last semester in college. My plan was to pay these off and then save a little money to get a place of my own.

At first, I promised myself I would continue to look for a good legal job, one where they would compensate me well for my nine years of college. I would, of course, only consider one that paid what I was worth. I also promised myself that in any case I would not stay with the software company for longer than a year, because I had bigger expectations.

About four months after I had began working with this company, I decided to start visiting friends of mine from school. I went to Guatemala to visit a close friend and to attend his wedding. It was a fantastic experience. I did not understand much of what was said because my Spanish was less than basic, but I really did enjoy my week there.

About three weeks after returning from Guatemala, I ran into Ana, that cute Dominican girl I had become friends with at American University. I was on a sales trip to New York; she was in New York to take the bar exam. We discovered that I was working about ten minutes from her sister's apartment. We went out for dinner one evening and things went well.

After hearing about my recent trip to Guatemala, Ana invited me to visit her country if I ever wanted to. She had no idea I would love to take her up on the offer.

Three weeks to the day later, I was on a flight to visit Santo Domingo. She arranged my stay at Hotel Santo Domingo for the first few days, and we went with a group of friends to Punta Cana for the weekend. I was hooked!

My Second Visit to Santo Domingo

I enjoyed my first week-long trip to the DR so much that I decided I would try to visit as much as financially possible. I had plenty of free time because I was only consulting two weeks a month, and the company would fly me to a new location each time I went to work. I had a little extra money. Visiting was only a little more expensive than being at home, but it was way better than just going to my parents' basement. The Dominican Republic was quite close in relation to traveling from Utah each week. In fact, it was closer than most trips to the East Coast.

I scheduled my second trip to the DR about three weeks after my first visit. I stayed at Hotel Santo Domingo again, and because Ana's cousin worked there I got a family rate of something like $80 per night. It was great. I would spend around $500 each week on the hotel, which included an elaborate and delicious breakfast. We would eat lunch at the local restaurants (Pizzarelli, Provocon, the food court at Acropolis, the restaurant in *Supermercado Nacional, Av. Abraham Lincoln*), which cost around US$10 for both of us. For dinner, we went to nicer restaurants (Tony Roma's, Colonial District, TGI-Friday's, and Conuco are the ones that come to mind). Each trip was probably costing me around $800-$1000. In my opinion, I was spending close to what I would spend dating in the US, as far as the food costs were concerned.

The hotel bill was close to what I would have spent for rent. It was really quite easy to justify.

Meeting Ana's Family

During my second visit I met Ana's family. It was a weird experience: although by now I considered her my girlfriend, I was under strict orders to act like we were "just friends" – whatever that means. Besides, I didn't speak any Spanish, so how could I have said differently?

When we arrived in La Vega, I was in for a big surprise. Ana's family figured that my visit was a big event, so they all decided to show up. I mean *everyone* – brothers, sisters, their respective wives and husbands, nieces, nephews, cousins, aunties, uncles, and neighbors. To me it felt very overwhelming; as they spoke so quickly I never even picked up one word. In all, there were probably close to thirty people. It was like a family reunion. My girlfriend talked to everyone for me, but I had no idea what was going on. They would ask me questions and she would interpret. I would then answer and she would answer back. Since then, I have learned that this was not really any big event. Those same thirty people are there almost every weekend. Ana's mom demands that everyone come over to eat as much as possible.

One of the highlights of my first trip to La Vega was eating sugar cane and coconut for the first time. Sugar cane is very sweet, but has an aftertaste much like hay. You chew on sticks of the grainy, bamboo-like stalks of the plants. You suck the liquid out and then spit out the fibrous part. After eating sugar cane, the fresh coconut water and coconut was not very sweet, but it was a great experience. I still have pictures from that day with me drinking right from a green coconut. I had never eaten either of these things but was really excited to try them.

After the La Vega trip, my girlfriend and I decided it would be good to try to plan my visits on a regular basis. Her family had liked me because they could tell I treated her very well. It was very important to her that her family approve of me. She was worried about what they might think. To me there was nothing to worry about. I treated her well and with respect. Show me a family that would not appreciate that!

Ana was not much for planning; she just said I could visit whenever I wanted. She would help with the hotel reservations. I arranged the flights. It worked well. Her cousin would arrange my discounted rooms. Since then, there hasn't been a time longer than three weeks when I have not been in the Dominican Republic.

At about the same time, my girlfriend began to express the fact that she was worried about how much money I was spending. She said she would try to help me save money because "I would otherwise be broken". We started to eat at her house every Wednesday. We began to buy food and eat more and more at my hotel. What she was really doing was helping me become more like a local. As I changed my lifestyle from a tourist to a resident, we spent less and less money in restaurants. I'll go through these changes later in the book.

About My Job

A quick word of caution before you read this section: Do not let this section dissuade you from continuing to read the entire book. I have only included this part so my "story" sounds complete, as you read the lessons I have learned. One of my preliminary readers cautioned me about discussing my job because it sounded "perfect", or even "unachievable." In my opinion, the job is not what made me successful in my transition. My attitude did that. In addition, I will discuss income options later in the book and will continue to add other avenues of potential income to the book's website as things progress. Read this section about my job so you understand the amount of travel and my need to be flexible as I made the transition. We will discuss jobs, money, and income in subsequent sections.

Let's turn to my work. As I mentioned earlier, when I first graduated I thought I would be a big-shot lawyer one day. However, as I realized the staggering number of hours lawyers work and how much they end up getting paid per hour that idea became less and less appealing. I started to work with the software company for two reasons: Money and Schedule. They paid quite well and I was able to work a week-on, week-off schedule. It was my initial plan to work for them for a year, and use the weeks off to find my dream job in the legal field. As life went on, however, my desire to work as an international trade lawyer slowly faded.

My job consisted of conducting training seminars on Internet marketing and selling the company's software and services to the seminar attendees. I did not really know anything about Internet marketing when I started, so I just relied on my ability to talk with people. The seminars were presented by professional speakers who knew how to market on the Internet, and who had often done very well with Internet marketing in their past. My job was to get the people attending the seminar to buy the company's software. The job was easy. The worst part of the job was we worked really long days, with my alarm ringing at 6 AM and our travel and set-up for the next day concluding often around 11PM or later. I would typically travel to work on Sunday. We would work six days (Monday-Saturday) and I would fly home the following Sunday. It worked well.

During the week we were very busy, so there was not much time for anything else. I did very little preparation of my exit plan, or implementing ideas that would have helped me get out of that job one day.

One of the best parts of the job was that we were in a different location every week. We would find out where we were headed a week or so in advance, and then the team would go and do the seminars. We worked in teams of ten people. Most of the people lived in Utah, but occasionally the company would agree to fly someone from somewhere else. I knew of people from Colorado, Idaho, Nevada, and later on California, Atlanta, and New York who all worked for the company.

In this job I had the opportunity to visit most of the United States. I also visited Australia several times, Tasmania, every province in Canada, Korea and Malaysia. Traveling quickly became a way of life. I was either headed to the airport or I was headed home from the airport on just about any given day.

For many people, this amount of travel would

become old very quickly. In fact, the company had a turnover rate of about eight months for most employees. It seemed that people would just get to where they were beginning to know what to do and how to sell – and some sort of problem would arise in their lives, and they'd have to move on to something else. As a result, the company paid quite well to keep people on as long as possible.

In my situation, where I was beginning to visit the DR on my weeks off, the job became the perfect match for my need to make money while I was living in the Dominican Republic. I was making decent money, yet I was regularly free for an entire week. That enabled me to be able to fly out Sunday night to the DR and fly back to Utah Saturday night so I could meet up with my team on Sunday.

The first four months I went to the Dominican Republic, I literally took ten flights a week. Each time, I stayed in the Salt Lake City airport from the time my flight landed when I came home from work until my next flight took off for the DR. Coming back, I spent Saturday night with my family between returning from the DR and when my team left on Sunday. I got tired of this quickly.

I left several sets of clothing in Santo Domingo, so my suitcase would not be overloaded with both work clothes and my clothes for the week off. I kept them in an extra suitcase, either leaving it with the hotel or giving it to Ana to take home. I left my dirty socks, undershirts, and underwear each week to be laundered. I took my work clothes to the dry cleaner each week and picked them up before I left the following week. When I left Santo Domingo to go to work, I would put my dirty laundry in a laundry bag and have it laundered while I was working the next week. Ana would pick up the laundry and bring it to me when she picked me up at the airport. At first, I left roughly five outfits, one week's worth of undergarments and socks, and my running clothes. Probably in all they were only worth around $300.

After a couple of months of this crazy travel schedule, Ana and I decided it would be much better if I flew directly to and from wherever my team was headed. It would save me close to $600 per week, as well as giving me an extra day without travel. I could simply fly into and out of the DR each Sunday. The problem as I saw it was how to approach the company, and how to let them know I wanted to move to the Dominican Republic. Ana did not feel I was actually *moving* to the DR. She saw my weekly appearances as visits, because I always left at the end of each week. My company, on the other hand, would see this as a move, because I would be permanently flying out of Santo Domingo, rather than Salt Lake City. I called it "my move". She still wasn't convinced I'd continue to come back each week.

Luckily, I had a very supportive manager. He had been to the Dominican Republic on a service mission and absolutely loved the country. He was really excited that I was considering moving. After talking things over with my manager, and with his approval and support, I decided to schedule a meeting with the VP of our company to ask about my changed travel location. I said I needed to talk with him about some issues, and that I probably needed half an hour to meet with him. I was apprehensive because I didn't want him to refuse me outright. And I was nervous, not knowing how long I would be physically able to maintain this amount of traveling.

When we met, I explained I had been flying each week to the DR, and that I wanted to move there. I told

him about my experiences and how excited I was to
be able to meet my girlfriend every week off. He had
recently been to the DR and had bought a condo in Juan
Dolio. He was crazy about the place. In fact, many of
the upper management had bought condos in the same
project. I explained I would like to have the company
book my flights directly from the DR each week and
wanted to get his permission. He said, "No problem –
I'll just send an email to the travel agent." We were only
about five minutes into our meeting. Up to now, it just
felt like chit-chat conversation; my manager didn't seem
bothered at all by what I had to say.

Then he became more serious, as though he
thought this was the beginning of a long meeting. "What
was it you really needed to talk with me about?" he asked.
Now he was the one who seemed nervous!

I told him I only wanted to talk with him about my
flight schedule. I explained how worried I had been that
the company would not agree, and how tough the travel
had been on me the past couple of months. He reassured
me that there was no problem, and that the company
would do what was necessary to keep me onboard. "It's
possible, though," he said, "we might have to ask you to
pick up the extra airfare from time to time, if your ticket
costs become too expensive." I gladly agreed; after all, I
would now be saving almost $1500 per month.

We stayed with that arrangement for just under
four years. I rarely had to pay for a ticket out of pocket,
although I did use some free sky miles from time to time.
I also have paid exchange fees a couple of times, and
occasionally some fees for overweight baggage. The move
was easy. I was now living in the Dominican Republic.
That's what I told my friends and family. I think most

people thought I was just going on vacation each week. Whatever they wanted to think was fine with me. I didn't care: as far as I was concerned, I had moved.

It was about this time I really began to realize the impact of moving to the Dominican Republic. Now I would be unable to do the things I usually did on my weeks off. I would no longer be able to go shopping in American stores whenever I wanted. There would be no Wal-Mart just down the street for daily necessities. I was out of reach of a good running store. I was literally living in a foreign country, and a third world country at that. I was living the expatriate lifestyle, but with the added benefit of frequent visits to American shopping.

I learned to take advantage of every opportunity to purchase certain items that are impossible to obtain in the DR. I would plan ahead to take an extra suitcase to make a special purchase in a given week. I bought power bars, American gum, and energy supplements for my running.

It was the beginning of my metamorphosis into a Dominican.

My First Lessons

I am including two sections about the various things I learned, because I think there really are several levels of lessons you learn, as you become an expatriate. This first section covers the more basic areas. These lessons will be of benefit to you while you are still green, even when you're just a tourist. I hope my experiences will give you a better foundation on which to build, and help you avoid mistakes I made when I was first visiting the DR. I'll begin each lesson with a rule or some guidelines, and then provide some stories or background to explain why each lesson is so significant. Some of the most important lessons will cover:

- How to deal with the perception of being an outsider, and mitigating any potential risks caused by this perception.

- How Dominicans think about money.

- How to deal with the social and societal distinctions between living in a first-world country and living in a third-world country.

I will not discuss security in this section because I have given security and safety a separate section of their own. Security, in my opinion, is one of the most critical areas of consideration as you visit or move to a new country. I want to begin with the most important principles I have learned as a traveler:

1. Always exhibit confidence!

2. The Dominican view of money and how to protect what you have.

3. How to make purchases, especially larger purchases.

4. Adjusting to unfamiliar living conditions and related lifestyle changes.

5. Staying in touch with your life through the Internet and international calling.

6. Living in a world where it is normal not to understand

everything that is going on around you, and using it to your advantage.

Always Exhibit Confidence!

One of the biggest and most helpful lessons I have learned as I have been in and out of the Dominican Republic is the fact that many people have no idea what is going on, not even the authorities. I remember speaking with a guy who had traveled in and out of the DR for close to twenty years. He said the officials in the airport were mainly uneducated or poorly-educated flunkies, many of whom got their jobs because they "knew someone". He said many of them could not read; and they were all worried about making sure their bosses or other higher ranked officials did not get upset with them. He explained that the jobs in the airport were well-paying jobs and were highly sought after.

With that in mind, he taught me how to be in control when dealing with almost anyone in the airport. He said he never allowed anyone but the Immigration officials to question him. He would not stop at the person who collects Customs forms after he cleared Immigration. He would simply hand the Customs officer his filled-in and stamped card, and then walk through. The more confidence he showed, the less they would ask.

He also said he never waited in line at the airport. The key was the amount of confidence he expressed in his knowledge that what he was doing was absolutely the right thing to do. His confidence helped him both in the airport and in his dealings with Dominicans in everyday life. He felt Dominicans could tell he was sure of himself, and that confidence earned him more respect; but he also said he was never unfair and was definitely not arrogant, because those traits would make people resentful.

For starters, it is important to understand clearly the process of entering a foreign country. Whenever you enter a country, you have to clear both Immigration and Customs. Immigration officials determine whether you physically can enter the country. This is the entrance for your person. Customs officials determine whether the stuff you bring with you is allowed to enter the country, and whether you have to pay any duties or taxes. Customs will not allow you to enter with certain prohibited items and they will charge you duties or taxes if you bring too much of one thing. The Immigration officer is the one you talk to first, who will always look at your passport. They will run your information through their computer and make sure you are entitled to enter. They will stamp your passport and your Customs card. After you pick up your luggage from the baggage carrousel, you give the stamped Customs card to the Customs official as you leave the secure area. This process is almost always identical, no matter which country you enter.

In the Dominican Republic, the Customs official is supposed to determine (based on some obscure set of observations) whether your belongings should be searched for possible items that should be taxed. The search is conducted by running your bags through an X-ray machine, and then afterwards by a hand search. They look for items like electronics in boxes (*e.g.*, televisions, flat screens, computers, etc.).

They also look for individuals who are transporting more than the normal quantity of luggage. This one is interesting, because most Dominicans carry many bags, particularly when they are entering the Dominican Republic. Dominicans who are going to the island to visit bring gifts for friends and family. Dominicans who are returning from a trip abroad bring back bags and bags of new stuff they bought while they were out of the country.

The key here is simply to hand the Customs official your paper and continue to walk. Make them stop you if they want to ask you questions. In four years of entering the country weekly I have been searched twice, once when I brought a bicycle and the other when I brought a very large picture frame. Neither of these stops ended with me paying any duties, because I expressed absolute confidence that the items I was bringing were allowed without a tax. The bike I brought cost roughly US$4,000, but they did not know that. I explained that it was an old bike I needed to use here to keep in shape. The bike was in pieces and they didn't know the difference. No problem. During the past four years, I have brought in hundreds of different items to the country, including vanities for my residence, and have not paid any duties.

When you leave a country, the process is almost exactly opposite of entering. The US does not ask Americans for anything when they leave. The US does require foreigners to turn in a little white card (I-94) saying they are leaving, but there are no exit stamps on the passports. When leaving the Dominican Republic you will first clear Security. You need to fill out a Customs form that is collected just prior to going through Security (this has only recently become necessary). After you clear Security, you need to turn in your Immigration form to the Immigration official. Once you are done in Immigration, you are free to go to your gate. There is usually someone directing you to the proper gate.

Let's turn to some of my lessons about the presence of confidence. I believe many of the lines and other obstacles created by ordinary travelers are senseless. Soon after I learned this little tidbit about confidence, I decided to try my luck bypassing the entire check-in line. At that time, the Delta ticket counter in the Santo Domingo airport did not have a First Class/Elite Access Line. One day when I arrived later than I had intended, there were close to 300 people lined up back and forth way past the little check-in lanes we are all used to. The customers had decided it was a good idea to make the line kind of weave all the way to the front door. When I entered the airport the number of people lined up to check-in blew me away. It was almost as if the ticket agents had asked everyone for all the flights that day to show up before they decided to start checking them in.

After seeing the line and determining it would take me at least two hours to get through it, I decided it was a good day to test my luck skipping the line. I was definitely not going to just get in line without at least giving it a shot. I thought it was a better idea to try to skip the line, so I simply went around the side and walked up to the front. I waited for the next agent and just walked to the counter with my passport out. The security guard tried to stop me, but I told him that it was all right because I was a Platinum frequent flyer with Delta and I did not need to wait in the line. It worked, because the security guard quickly took my bag and put it on the scale for me. He also told the ticket agent I was a special customer. Some of the people in the line did not like what happened, but the security guard told them it was all right because I was a special passenger. Little did he know! The young lady at the ticket counter was very friendly. She thanked me for being a good customer and made sure my First Class seat was just right. She also helped me upgrade to First Class for my entire trip, at no additional charge. I mean, who wouldn't want to help out a special flyer that didn't need to wait in lines?

About a month later, Delta installed a First Class/ Elite check-in line. I have never waited in a long line again. I ask people standing in the First Class/Elite line if they are First Class, and if not, I just go in front of them.

For a while, I even got the security guard to walk me around the side in front of everyone, even those passengers waiting in the First Class/Elite check-in line, and get me the next open agent. Delta has changed things lately; but for a long time my confidence worked so well I could get in front of the line no matter what. A couple of times I even got the security guard to take my passport to the agent at the counter and return with my ticket. I would *never* wait in line.

One of my most memorable experiences when my confidence paid off was when my flight was canceled because of a hurricane. Almost immediately, all the people waiting at the gate rushed the gate counter. There was a very long line and lots of yelling and questioning. I quietly went backwards through the Immigration and Customs area. I told them I needed to go out front to change my ticket. When I arrived out front there were not very many people, so I just went directly to the counter where the agent had helped me about 30 minutes before. Yes, I skipped the line. I walked right in front of people because I was in dire need of getting to work. I told the security guard to keep the people back. He did his job perfectly.

The agent said the other flight was full, but he could bump someone flying standby if I was willing to take a middle seat in the back. I said, "Give me whatever you've got. I REALLY appreciate it." By the time the ticket agent had changed my ticket and given me my seat on the new flight, there were several hundred people lined up to get their new tickets. There were many more people than just those who were flying, because by that time many friends and family were showing up at the airport to assist their stranded comrades. The agent said I needed to hurry back through Security but that he would meet me inside with all of my ticketing information. I used my original ticket (from the canceled flight) to go back through Security and went to the gate of the other flight. The agent from out front was now working at the gate for the new flight inside Security. Of course, I asked if he was able to get me First Class. He said he'd check – and before I could even imagine it, I had a First Class seat on an oversold flight!

As I shook the ticket agent's hand thanking him for getting me on the flight, I slipped him US$20. I also later gave the security guard a PSP video he wanted. Those two little "thank yous" are the only things I have ever given anyone at the airport, but my thankfulness has paid off many times over. Through my confidence and my new friends, I have been able to help visiting friends and family bypass ticketing lines. I have been able to help friends and family upgrade to First Class (because I am a Frequent Flyer), even when I am not personally flying. For about two years, I could get people upgraded to First even when they traveled on an awards ticket, even when I was not physically flying with them on the flight; but that is getting much more difficult recently, since the Delta/

Northwest merger.

I have learned to use my confidence. I know the agent is just doing his or her job and they want to keep clients happy, particularly "special clients." With this confidence and new perspective, I have been able to obtain many advantages. I always treat people working in the airport with complete respect. I ask them to help me with something and I make sure to thank them when they do what I need. I also make sure to go out of my way to say, "Hi! Good to see you!" every time I get a chance. You never know when a flight will be canceled or when you'll be stuck in a middle seat in the back.

It has been almost two years since I have flown coach on Delta. Yes, in my opinion, Delta is the best airline for travel to and from the Dominican Republic. They treat me well. They give me upgrades. They usually do not experience delays. (I'll go into more detail when I discuss the other airlines and their advantages and disadvantages later on in the book).

The Dominican View of Money

Almost immediately upon landing on my first trip to Santo Domingo, I started being taught lessons about how differently people act and deal with money in the DR. In fact, before I had even left the airport I had the opportunity to give money to several people. First, I was approached at the baggage carousel inside Customs and asked if I needed help with my bags. I mean, seriously: I traveled for work every Sunday. I was used to shipping tons of boxes and luggage. For this flight I had one suitcase. I got rid of that guy fairly easily.

Second, I was approached in Customs as I was answering the questions about what I had in my bag. (If you follow the instructions from the previous section, you won't deal with these questions). Once again, this was a porter asking if I needed help out with my bags. NO, thank you.

Third, as I left Customs and was approached by multiple *taxistas* (guys who work for the taxi companies) to see if I needed a ride. Once again, "NO;" I had arranged transportation ahead of time.

Fourth, did I need help carrying my bag from the door to the car? Or would I like help putting the bag into the car? Some of these guys don't even ask if you want or need their help. They just come and try to take the bag from you. I have almost lost it several times. I always look at them like they are stealing my bag and hold on very sternly. And say "NO" confidently. They go away quickly once they realize you are not going to just let them start helping you.

My girlfriend taught me the most important lesson with regard to money. I learned the lesson because I was a little too gullible, at least that's what she thought. On my second trip to the Dominican Republic, just after I left the main terminal I realized I did not see Ana. I looked for her in the agreed-upon spot and found a place to wait. After a few minutes, I decided it would be best just to call her and figure out where she was. The dilemma was that I needed to call her but did not have a cell phone that worked. At the time, my US cell phone had not been set up for international calls, so it wouldn't pick up any signal. I did what you would usually do in the USA. I asked a security guard where I could find a *telefono*, figuring I could find a payphone and call her from there. He acted very sure and turned to a guy about two feet away and told him to give me his cell phone. The guy dialed the number into his phone and handed it to me. When the call was over, he told me I needed to give him five dollars. I had figured I would have to pay him something, but even an expensive call shouldn't be more than a dollar. I said "Yeah, right!" and gave him three dollars, because that was what came out of my pocket when I grabbed the small wad of bills. I thought that was a little expensive, but I really needed to figure out where Ana was waiting for me. Besides, the security guard directed me to that guy, so that was probably how he made his living. It was a little weird, but it worked. When my girlfriend and I found each other, she asked how I called her. After I explained how I used someone's cell phone, she gave me my first lesson in dealing with Dominicans with regard to money.

As we were driving to drop my things off at my hotel, she explained that most Dominicans believe all Americans have tons of money. She said I really needed to be careful with money, because people could easily tell I was not Dominican and would take advantage of me. She gave me some general suggestions to follow and I have since made them hard and fast rules. The rules are as follows:

1. Unless I am making a specific purchase, I do not give money to anyone, no matter what.

2. I do not give spare change to people for whom I feel sympathy – not poor-looking children who need food, not beggars in the street with their children in tow, not window washers, none of them, no matter how badly mangled their bodies are. (After seeing "Slumdog

Millionaire", I think I understand why so many
are mangled beyond belief!)

3. I do not give money to her, her family, her
   friends, or her acquaintances, no matter what;
   and

4. If I am ever in doubt, I refer to rule #1 – Do not
   give money to anyone!

After living here for the past four years, I look
back on my first experiences with money in the DR. I am
grateful for Ana's wisdom in explaining the Dominican
view of money. She probably did not know how helpful
her advice would be to me. Looking back, she really knew
what advice would protect me from possible harm, as
well as protect me from potentially-awkward situations.
    Let me explain the money situation a little further.
The Dominican society is one where poor people often
feel they have a right, or maybe even a duty, to try to get
money from the people who have more money than they
do. Many learn this as children, when their parents give
them 20 pesos once a week or so to go and buy candy.
They quickly learn that their *Tia* (Aunt) or *Tio* (Uncle)
will give them money sometimes just because they look
cute or when they do something good. They also learn
to ask for money from family members and close friends.
All too often, these people will give in to their begging
and hand them a few pesos.
    The difference between a good family and a
family of beggars is that the good family will not allow
the children to ask others outside the family for money.
My wife Ana comes from a good family: not one member

of her family has ever asked me for money, not even a dime. My wife gets asked, but I am off limits. A family of beggars allows their children to continue to ask, and in some cases even takes their children to convenient places to ask strangers for money. In the Dominican Republic, the corrupt government feeds beggar mentality. Even public servants feel empowered to ask for handouts. Once governmental employees feel that it is all right to ask for a handout, it is surely all right for poor people to ask. When there are enough poor people asking for handouts, the tide shifts and there is almost an obligation for the person with money to give. I have seen situations where the beggar acted as if the person with money owed the beggar a debt. I have a hard time with this. I tip well for low-income workers who do a good job, but I do not give freebies.

Tourists, visitors, and charity workers are often targets because they are known to have money, and often are very vulnerable because they also have soft hearts. These individuals feel an extra bit of self-inflicted pressure not normally felt by locals. The pressure begins when these individuals are touched or feel some sort of guilt because they have so much more than the poor folks they see on the corners. I think this a self-inflicted pressure because these individuals often think they are doing something noble when they hand a few pesos to a beggar. They think they are going to change someone's life because they are giving them something for free. What they do not realize is that many of the beggars make their living feeding on these emotions. It is a vicious cycle.

I have heard stories of tourists getting a ride in a hotel taxi or renting a car and going into very poor neighborhoods just to hand out money. I was told first-

hand by a visitor that he had given several thousand dollars
out during his weeklong visit to the DR. He literally had
a driver take him to a poor area and handed $20 bills to
the kids on the street. The kids mobbed his car so badly
the second time he went into one particular neighborhood
that he was worried they might start ripping parts off the
car. I think he's lucky he didn't have any major problems.
His justification was he wanted to do something that
would have an impact on the poor people. He felt that
handing out money to each of the poor children would in
some way help their families be better.

I think there are too many people like this guy who
think they are doing something good or something that
will help the poor. In reality, they are creating a bigger
problem. They are teaching people they can get something
for nothing. I always refer back to Rule #1: Never give
people money in exchange for nothing. When I want to
give money, I give it to a church or an organization that
will really do something to have an impact on the lives
of the poor. I do not give it to some kid who will end
up giving it to his dad to buy a *Presidente*, which is the
national beer and a pride of the Republic.

Just so you don't get the idea that I have never
been naïve, I will finish this lesson with a story about a
time when I was taken by a guy in Customs at the airport.
At the time I was leaving the DR to go back to the USA, I
was stopped by an official in the Immigration area at the
airport in Santo Domingo. I had gone through the metal
detectors that lead into the Immigration area, but had not
gotten to the counters where you give the Immigration
official your passport and paperwork. As I left the Security
area and began to head toward Immigration, an official-
looking gentleman asked me for my passport. He had on

some sort of badge and was dressed in slacks and a sport coat. Since I was still relatively new to the Immigration and Customs thing, my guard went up; but I agreed to let him look at my passport. After he looked at it and determined that I had been visiting fairly often lately, he told me I had overstayed my visa. He explained that he was going to have to take my passport. He said I needed to pay a fine and he could personally accept the penalty.

Now, I was born at night, but not last night. This guy was trying to get some money from me and he thought I was just stupid enough to give him whatever he wanted. I quickly determined that I had to figure out the best way out of the situation and fast. I told him I did not have any cash on me, but if we could go to an ATM I would get cash. I said, "I don't want any problems, so let me through and I'll find an ATM." He said he would let me through, but not to mention my problem to the agent at the counter or they would likely keep me for questioning. I got it. "Keep quiet and you will be all right. After you go and get money, I will find you inside and you can give it to me." I understood perfectly.

After clearing Customs, I immediately went to the food stand and got a Coke. I went directly there because I figured he wouldn't be able to follow me closely or quickly. Lots of other people were there, too, and I was betting he would not want to give me a hard time in front of them. I paid with my American Express card (see purchasing recommendations below), and as I put my wallet away, I took all my cash out and slipped it into my front pocket. I only left RD$200 (about US$6) in my wallet.

As I left the stand I noticed "my new friend" down the hall. I went immediately into the restroom, hoping he hadn't noticed me. No such luck. It just so happened that we were both washing our hands at the same time. I figured it was best to let him ask for the money, so I acted as if I didn't recognize him. As soon as I was finished washing my hands and beginning to dry them, he said, "Mister, I am hungry. They do not pay me enough to eat well. Give me some money so I can go get some food." I responded that there were no ATMs inside Security, so I could not get any cash. I told him I was hungry too, so I would give him half of what I had. His face lit up. As I opened my wallet and he saw there were only *pesos*, the smile slowly went away. He got RD$100. I kept the other RD$100. I told him to buy some food, and then I added "*Mi esposa abogada. No pregunta dinero más. Ella hablar con jefe.*" (My wife is lawyer. No ask money more. She talk with boss).

Remember in the previous section how every airport employee is concerned with their superior remaining happy? Well, I have since been through Customs and Immigration more than two hundred times, and have never been asked for money again. I have also not seen the guy again, probably because someone else who actually knew Spanish really did talk to his boss. I got taken, but not nearly as badly as I could have been.

As a *gringo* living in the DR, I am marked for life as a person who has more money than most people. When we go out in public I am a constant target for beggars, shoeshine boys, poor children, the maimed, and police. At first it was bothersome. After learning there are simple rules of money, and how to explain them without being insulting, I have not had any problems. Yes, I have broken the rules on occasion. I give money once every couple of months to a beggar child, particularly when I see one who seems too innocent for me to keep a stone-cold heart. I give money every now and then to the guardian at our apartment building, particularly when he goes out of his way to do something nice for us like washing our car. I tip well, and for good service I give extra and tell them why. With regard to friends and family, Ana deals with them. I sometimes have to tell her to give people money; but other than that, I follow the rules.

How to Make Purchases

For years I have been fanatic about never carrying any cash. In fact, before visiting the DR for the first time, I had become quite accustomed to going without cash and only using credit or debit cards to pay for everything. I have traveled quite a lot around the US and have never had a problem paying with a credit card. Because some stores do not accept American Express, I carry a Visa card as a backup.

Dominicans are quite different from North Americans in that they are quite accustomed to paying for everything with cash. Ana pays our mortgage payment each month in cash (RD$35,000). To me, it seems weird to pay a bank in cash; but in the Dominican Republic, it is totally normal, because most transactions are made in cash. I have seen Dominicans who are just ordinary people carry the equivalent of thousands of dollars in cash with them.

Living in the Dominican Republic for several years has led me to believe it is good always to carry a little cash, but never a lot. I think around RD$1000 ($US28) is about right. If you need more money, you can always visit an ATM. When I need cash, I withdraw money from big banks' machines. I do not use unmarked machines. I usually know when I am going to need to spend more than RD$1000 on any given day, so I plan my purchases a little in advance so as to have enough cash handy.

I still try to make my larger purchases with a credit card. I do so for several reasons. First, I use cards that offer me free miles for travel. I accumulate miles for whenever my wife or family is going to travel, and I use them to buy these tickets. (I personally try not to fly on a rewards ticket. It seems counterproductive, since I can accumulate so many miles by buying a regular ticket. See the travel section below for more information on this.)

Second, most credit cards have some sort of guarantee or protection for fraud and other non-authorized charges. In the past four years, I have had one such experience: the hotel where I stayed double-charged me. A quick call to American Express took care of that. I also had one erroneous deduction from my checking account. The error happened when I tried to withdraw money from an ATM, but the machine did not give me any money. Once again, a quick call to my bank returned the money to my account. Finally, I like credit cards because they are easy to track; and if you need to deduct any charges for tax purposes, they are easy to follow.

I prefer using American Express, because American Express gives me the best rewards and they seem to have the best customer protection. Let me use our furniture purchases as an example. After we bought our house, we needed to purchase everything, since neither Ana nor I had anything. We needed appliances for the kitchen and the laundry. We needed beds, furniture for our living room, a table and chairs for our dining room, and a desk for my office. I moved to the Dominican Republic in a suitcase, so my belongings were severely limited.

Ana had been living in her brother's house as a guest for years, so she only owned clothing. As we shopped for furniture, it quickly became apparent that we were going to spend a lot of money. We did the math, and we figured it would end up costing us somewhere around US$30,000 to furnish our apartment with the basics. Furniture was more expensive in Santo Domingo that I was used to in the US, but what are you going to do? There were credit options; but to me, the interest rates were obnoxious, and I preferred to get the Sky Miles.

We decided to negotiate the best prices we could with the sales people. My wife and I would go one day and look at things. She would then go back another day and negotiate on her own, or with her brother. It seemed they could get better deals not having the *gringo* in tow. They would negotiate the price for cash, no financing needed, and then we would pay with my American Express card. I would get the Sky Miles, and we would have the best price possible.

Soon after we purchased our kitchen table, we noticed that one of the chairs had a crack in the leg. It wasn't bad enough to bother us at first, so we left it. About four months later, I noticed that the table was not perfectly flat. It had kind of a curve in the middle, which I did not remember seeing before. I looked underneath and noticed that the support on one side was not attached properly. I tried to screw the screws in better, but they were stripped out and wouldn't tighten. I told my wife about the problem, but we did not take immediate action. Over the next couple of months, we watched the table proceed to get worse. The support eventually hung down about four inches, and the table had a noticeable bow in the middle. Apparently, the table was not going to fix itself; we would have to go to the furniture store to remedy the problem. We repeatedly went to the store where we had purchased the table, but no one there was willing or able to help us. We kept being referred from one person to another. It was ridiculous. We had spent thousands of dollars in this store; but the only people available would happily assist us to make a purchase, but none of them could help us with our problem. The salespeople simply did not discuss problems with already-purchased furniture. As soon as we mentioned the problem, we were told the manager was out of the store. We were given a phone number to call. We were given every possible reason why they could not fix the problem immediately.

After several fruitless tries at asking the store's customer service department for help, my wife decided it was time to confront the salesman who had initially helped us. The sales guy began by giving us the same sort of runaround we had been getting from the customer service department. He, however, was not as good at deflecting us, and quickly referred us to the store's warehouse just down the street. According to him, the store manager's office was in the warehouse. He even gave us the name of a person who could authorize the exchange.

When we first arrived at the warehouse, the staff was more than helpful. They asked for our receipt and were ready to load our new purchase into our vehicle. As soon as we explained that we were trying to fix a problem with a previously-purchased item, the individual we were referred to was less than cordial. He even had the nerve to imply that we must be using the table improperly. In any case, he was sure that it was not their fault. He said the warranty was gone. Regardless of what the problem was, we were responsible for dismantling the table and bringing it to the store for him to see before he could authorize any work. In any case, we would have to pay for the labor. As I listened, my blood began to boil. My poor wife had to deal with this jerk, while her English-speaking husband stood there and watched like an idiot.

Just as I was ready to snap, the light clicked on in my head. I PAID WITH MY AMEX! I interrupted the conversation and said, "Excuse me, do you understand English?" The guy responded that he knew a few words. "Good," I said. "Listen, I paid with my American Express card. If you don't fix this *now,* I will call them and charge the transaction back. Understand?"

Of course, he didn't understand English well enough, so I used my best Spanish. It was probably a thousand times better than this guy's English anyway! I said something like, "I bought everything for our house here and paid with my American Express card. If you don't take care of this today, I am going to call them and have them give me my money back for everything. I won't pay for any of it. I don't want to fight you about this, but if you want to fight, I will let you fight American Express." His tone changed almost immediately.

The funny thing about American Express is that I really have no idea what they would have said about a six-month-old transaction. Would they really give the merchant a hard time about the table? I don't know. The beauty of it all was – he didn't know what American Express would do either. Most merchants in the US would have no idea, let alone Dominican merchants. After he heard my threat, the guy immediately stopped yelling. He blew out a big breath and rubbed his head. He walked behind the counter and looked at some sort of list. He called a driver and had the driver follow us to our house to pick up the table. Within ten minutes of the threat, they were inside my house taking the table apart. Within thirty minutes, the table and broken chair were headed back to the store.

I tipped the driver and his helper well (RD$100, about US$3 each), so they would be happy about coming back. About four days later the driver called my wife and said he needed to deliver our table and chair. When he arrived, he said that since the original ones were broken, he had just gotten us a brand-new pair. What really happened? I have no idea. All I know for sure is that I finally got what I paid for – a brand-new table and a brand-new chair. Ana is sure the driver had no authority to give us the new table. I agree.

I will always make my larger purchases with my American Express card. It is the one thing I hold in the bargaining that no one can mess with. It's the wild card I can use later if I ever need to fight about quality. I'm a big fan!

Living Conditions and Lifestyle Changes

Making the move from a first-world country to a third-world country requires some adjustments to lifestyle and living conditions. When I first moved, I lived in a nice hotel and always had hot running water. For a long time this was something I took for granted. I also always had electric power twenty-four-seven, and rarely dealt with the power outages endured by the locals. I had air conditioning and all the amenities you would expect at a nice American hotel. As a result, I really did not encounter or have to adjust to many of the country's infrastructure problems at first. Let's consider several of the most apparent disparities between the American and the Dominican ways of life.

Electricity. At first, all I really noticed about the electricity was the poorly-maintained infrastructure. Often I saw dozens of wires running across the street – not the heavy-duty wires that carry power in the US, but smaller wires, like those normally used for indoor or conduit purposes. The first times I noticed the lower-grade electrical system were the continual power outages in malls or other public places. I cannot remember being in a US mall when the power has gone out. I assume that if the power went out in an American mall, the mall would just close. They would simply ask everyone to go home and come back when there was power. In the DR, a power outage is nothing to be bothered about. People don't even act as if anything unusual has happened. The cash registers run on battery power and it's "business as usual".

I remember one party at a friend's house. Everyone was singing and dancing. The music was loud. There were fans going to keep people cool. And then all of a sudden, the power went out, and the night was pitch-black. The song never even missed a beat; everyone kept singing, and someone kept time by banging on a plastic chair. The host turned to an end table and lit a candle. It was after the candle lit the room back up that I noticed the dancing had continued without any pause. The guitar... people singing... the dancing... everything just kept going as if the radio were still playing in the background. It was just part of normal life.

Bottled Water. While I was living in DC, I became quite sick with some strange headaches. I went to the medical center at the school, I went to a doctor, and I went to a neurologist. They were never able to identify the problem. However, during the course of these headaches, I read a news article about the high levels of lead in the DC water, and the resulting toxicity of the water. Following the article's recommendations, I stopped drinking tap water and started only drinking bottled water. Sometime afterwards my headaches went away. I don't know for sure that the lead was a cause of the headaches, but I have never since drunk from a tap. I always stop and buy water.

As a result, when I started visiting the DR it was not difficult for me not to drink the tap water. As far as I know, every Dominican family drinks bottled water. Also, most Dominican hotels give you bottled water in your room. One of the most troublesome things initially was to learn to use bottled water to brush my teeth. I even made it a point always to have Listerine in my bag, so I could use it as water when brushing my teeth if no bottled water was available. I have read that you need to be careful not to let water get into your mouth when you shower. I worried about that for about ten minutes once, but the fear is long gone.

Street Vendors. When you first visit the DR, you'll be shocked at what you can buy from street vendors. You might expect to see such wares as phone cards, ice cream, bottled water, cell-phone chargers, CD holders, steering-wheel covers, flowers, reading glasses, sun glasses, and new windshield wipers. I have also seen quite curious items being sold by the street vendors as well: for example, dogs, cats, birds, fish (yes, they carry the fish in a bowl or jar or plastic bag), television holders (the clamps that hold the TV high up on the wall), flags, hats, belts, shoes, cheese, bread, jumping ducks, kites, kids' toys, posters of every type, stickers, and just about any kind of fruit or vegetable you can imagine. Some of the fruit is already cut so you can just eat it. Other fruit is sold whole, so you can go home and prepare it. Name something, and you can probably buy it somewhere in the street from a vendor. If you want cheese, you just grab it from the tray. There is a stick stuck in it so you don't have to touch it with your fingers.

After several years of living in the Dominican Republic, I've realized that the rule for buying from street vendors depends on whom you listen to. I personally think most of the people are too dirty even to let their hands touch my hand. Most of the food looks way less than edible to me, and if I buy shoes or a belt I want to try them on for a while. If I get a new dog I want to see it walk around. So, other than phone cards, I do not buy from street vendors. To me, the transaction is too quick; and my car window is down, so I am not 100% comfortable.

Ana buys *limoncillos* and sometimes other fruits from vendors. I hate it when she bites into things she bought from some vendor on the street. I always make fun of the fruit and say the guy's dog probably peed on it; but she's so used to eating that stuff that she doesn't care. Many of our Dominican friends agree with me that the transactions are less than hygienic and can sometimes be dangerous.

For me, I will buy fruit from a fruit stand, but I prefer to go to the supermarket. I will buy a phone card on the street, but my doors are locked and my window is only partway down. I don't buy anything else from the street.

I remember a story about the homemade candy the

street vendors carry around in plastic tubs. The plastic tubs are chock-full of candy, and they carry the tubs on top of their heads. The tubs are filled so far above the rim they look as if they are about ready to fall over. I have never tasted the candy, but Ana has, and says it is rather bitter. One of our close friends told me it has a little "sweat of Haitian" in it that gives it a bitter taste. Our friend explained that they make the candy by hand. Since it is always hot here and the candy-maker is doing hard physical work, a little of the maker's sweat always gets into the candy. The sweat addition is something that just adds to the taste, hence the "sweat of Haitian" because the vendors and preparers are all Haitians.

I once thought I would eventually try that candy, but after hearing that story, I think it will be a long time before I do. I can't bear thinking about eating something that has some dude's sweat dripped in it, even if it does enhance the flavor! I try to keep that vision out of my mind, even though I know I probably have eaten sweat-enhanced food more than once...

International Calling and the Internet

As soon as you decide you are going to be calling the Dominican Republic a lot, you'll learn how expensive international calls can be. You have to be a little careful, because you can call the DR from any phone in the US with long distance by just dialing 1, the area code, and the number, exactly as if you were calling a number in the USA. The problem is that you will be charged international rates. I have seen the charges range from $.10 to $1.50 per minute. My cell-phone provider was one of the worst. They allowed me to have international calling, but they charge me for text messages, incoming calls, voice mails, everything. I have had months where my bill was over $300, and that was with me trying not to use the international roaming.

As a result, I have tried just about every option for international calling. One of the great things about the Internet is the vast number of Voice over Internet Protocol (VoIP) phone options. I have found two options that work just about perfectly. The first is Skype. The second is Magic Jack. Both options require you to have Internet access. You pay an annual small fee, and you get a US phone number where people can call you.

As far as my phone needs go, I currently have three numbers where I can be reached: US Cell, DR Cell, and VoIP. The US Cell phone number is the same phone number I've had for about ten years. I keep the basic plan that costs me around $50 per month. I get something like 1500 minutes, unlimited nights, and weekends. Whenever I am in the DR I forward the phone to my VoIP number, and I receive all the calls on my computer.

I have been through many different options over the past couple years, and this works the best. My DR Cell number is just a pre-paid cell phone. It works very well, but I really don't use it for much other than to call my wife. It probably costs me $20 per month to maintain it. I just buy cards to refill it when I run out of minutes. We also get a home phone number with my Internet service provider, so we have phones in our house. I rarely use the landline, except every now and then to call the corner store to order something.

The only real disadvantage with my current arrangement is that I have to maintain two numbers:

- <u>A US number</u>, which is really my US Cell phone number. I answer that phone when I am in the US and forward it to my computer when I'm in the DR; and

- <u>A DR number</u>, which is my DR Cell phone. I just turn the DR Cell phone off when I travel.

The Internet phone is on whenever the computer is on. With my account, it accepts voice mail, and sends me an email when I receive a voicemail; so even if I am offline, I am not out of touch. Sometimes I don't tell people where I am physically located. I have had people invite me to lunch or to have a meeting later in the day, thinking I'm just around the corner. In reality, I'm in an entirely different world.

"Not Understanding" Can Be an Advantage

I learned early on that not exactly understanding everything was not always a bad thing. Many of the conversations on the front porch, around the dinner table, and around town are quite simply senseless. "Not understanding" is another way to keep certain individuals away from you. Many people won't even try to talk with you if they think you don't understand. I do my best to use it to my advantage.

When Ana and I go shopping, I speak to her in English. Whenever I have people try to sell me something on the phone, I speak to them in English. I also encourage my wife to do most of the talking with sales people or when we have problems with the phone, Internet, or cable. It's nice for me not to have to deal with it. I also think there is an air of mystery about how much I really do know. Not understanding, or at least maintaining the impression that you do not understand, allows you to rely on your confidence and skills of reading people. It is sometimes a big advantage, because as you learn more and more Spanish, you will know which people are predators, and which are friends.

Here's an example of how it's an advantage not to know Spanish. Almost every day, I go for a run around Santo Domingo. I run a lot. As I run, people who want to sell me something often approach me. I get asked by beggars to give them money. Women wanting to sell me their services try to speak to me. Boys ask me if they can clean my running shoes. I simply act as if I cannot hear them; or I look at them and smile and nod as if I'm saying "hello" – but I say nothing. I cannot count the times they have said directly to my face, "He doesn't understand." I know it works, because they are speaking about me in the third person.

In fact, I've managed to train several people who could be complete nuisances. They are certain by now that I don't understand their Spanish at all. They often use a very loud tone when they try to talk with me, as if yelling at me will magically get me to understand Spanish. One of the most amusing ones is a watchman at my apartment building. He usually says *"Buenos días"* to me, but thinks I'm unable to understand anything he says. He tells sales people right in front of me not to bother trying to sell me anything, because I do not understand. I get a kick out of it.

For this to be an advantage, you cannot be seen as an idiot. You also must make sure you do not act arrogant. You have to understand enough of the language that people know you are trying to learn Spanish, even if it is only a simple *"Cómo tu 'ta?"* You've got to know some Spanish and use it; but you also have to know when it is better to just shut your mouth.

Using the yelling or speaking-slowly strategy doesn't work to teach them English, either. It amazes me when I see foreigners at the store or in the airport yelling in English or speaking really slowly. I feel like saying, "Dude, they speak *Spanish*. They are not deaf." As of this moment, while I'm writing this book, I haven't yet said that to any American, but now that I think of it, I'm going to use that one as soon as I get the chance!

When you use your foreignness to your advantage, keeping people in the dark on how much you really understand is a perfect situation to be in. Think back on my story about the table we bought and returned. One of the most important aspects of that story was that I allowed the manager to speak only with my wife, for quite a long time. I realized that he was speaking to her very sternly, almost rudely or aggressively, because he didn't think I understood what he was saying. I asked her if he was being too rude and she said it was all right. After a bit, it finally got to me, so I then tried to make him speak to me in English. In that case, I would then have been the one with the dominant language skills, which would have given me the better negotiating position. This strategy failed because his English was worse than my Spanish. As a result, I switched to Spanish, immediately letting him know I would not accept any further problems. He quickly realized that I knew exactly what was going on, and was not going to take any more of his condescending attitude. It worked perfectly: all he had seen up to that point was a non-Spanish-speaking guy who just stood by and listened. He obviously thought I was just another idiot foreigner who knew nothing and had tons of money.

One last example of when this strategy is perfect is when you need to cut in front of a line. When I want to cut in front of people who have formed a huge line, the fact that I am not "local" is an advantage. I remember going to a concert once. There was a line of about a hundred people waiting to buy a piece of pizza. I patiently waited in line until I was about ten feet from the counter. At that point, everyone started to push ahead and really crowd the counter. Since I am small, I figured I would get left behind if I didn't just push up front, which is exactly what I did.

The lady said, "Sir, you are not next. That man behind you is." I responded, "*'Ta bien, gracias* (I'm good thanks). I want four pieces of pizza and four Cokes."

She said to the guy behind me "Uh, I guess he doesn't understand. Let me take his order first and I'll take care of you next." I thanked the guy behind me and his wife. It worked perfectly.

I'm not going to wait any longer. I think next time I'll try to skip the line completely. When you don't understand, you can get away with a lot. Just don't be rude. Make sure you don't come across as an arrogant jerk. Act as if you are happy just to be there. For your lack of Spanish to be an advantage, you need to be sure you are never the idiot who insists on using English. Just keep quiet. Listen. Maintain the mystery. Life is good!

Lessons I Learned as I Became More Seasoned

For starters, do not consider this section to be "advanced" lessons. I have been here for about four years, and I still learn new things on a daily basis. I want you to think of this section as the lessons I learned while I became more consistent in my desire to be Dominican. The longer I am in the Dominican Republic, the more I desire to fit in and not be the *gringo* who stands out in a crowd. I can't change the way I look, but I can throw people off because I act Dominican. I love it when people ask whether I'm really Dominican!

These are the lessons I learned as I made the transition from questioning and observant tourist to expatriate, who wanted to fit in and be part of the surrounding culture.

1. My spending habits, and how I began to cut back on spending.
2. Issues I had with the police, and how I became invisible.
3. Buying a house or apartment and what to be aware of.
4. Getting a loan from a Dominican bank.
5. Exchanging money.
6. Dealing with window washers.
7. People who think I will give them stuff.
8. How to honk a horn properly.
9. Spanish classes.

How I Began to Cut Back on Spending

It probably took me about six months to realize that I needed to make a big change in my outlook on life, if I was to make a successful transition between being a tourist to becoming a local.

At first, every time I went to Santo Domingo I thought and acted like a visitor. I allowed myself to use my time as if I were on vacation. I stayed in a very nice hotel. I often spent money as if money didn't matter. Thinking back, I am surprised I made it through the transition, because I was used to spending freely. I guess initially I was both a little nervous about the new surroundings, and I didn't want to suffer from the everyday issues that were part of most locals' lives. I did not want to live without hot water and electricity available all the time. I had heard stories about problems with safety, so I was happy staying where there were lots of security and many tourists. I was also fairly content spending $1000 to $1500 each week for food, hotel, and entertainment. I was spending about two weeks each month in the Dominican Republic and I had no other bills, so $2000-$3000 was no big deal. I was living the Good Life.

My girlfriend and I talked at different times about what I needed to do if I was serious about living in the Dominican Republic. We began by talking about how often I would visit. I was serious enough about our relationship that I was ready to move. I was working every other week; so why shouldn't I spend my off weeks in the DR? Ana, on the other hand, felt that I needed to take it easy and adjust to things slowly.

Here's what she was worried about:
- the amount of money I was spending,
- my safety, and
- if I really did end up moving to Santo Domingo long-term, how I would deal with the differences between American and Dominican infrastructure.

She thought I would probably have a hard time dealing with hours and hours without power. She knew the humidity and heat were really difficult for me, particularly without air-conditioning. She also knew it would be tough for me to get used to taking cold showers, or bathing from a bucket when there is no water, which is often the case in typical Domingan life.

To begin with, we decided it would be best for me to stop staying at those expensive short-stay hotels, and move into a long-stay apart-hotel. Apart-hotels in Santo Domingo have a wide range of amenities. Some are very low budget. Others are very expensive. Over a period of around eight weeks Ana looked at many places. Some were not adequate because of issues like safety, Internet, or power. Others were way out of my price range. After about two months of looking, she found just the right place.

As we were considering various possible options for my new living space, we had several concerns. The main concern was security. Ana has been worried about my safety from the moment I arrived on my first visit. Second was the quality of Internet access. I worked for an Internet marketing company and needed to work on the Web almost daily. The Internet was one of my most-needed luxuries, and the Internet requires electricity. When the electricity turns off, the Internet goes as well. These two items were first and foremost in the things we looked for.

Another consideration was the location. I wanted to be close to libraries, supermarkets, and, of course, my girlfriend. I made it very clear from the beginning. I was here for her, and not because I wanted to be a tourist or because I liked the country. If we did not see each other at least every day, I would not come back.

I moved a few blocks from Hotel Santo Domingo to apart-hotel Plaza Florida, which was closer to Ana's workplace, anyway. The breakfast wasn't as good, but I saved a little money. The rooms had a desk, reliable Internet access, a kitchen, and the feel was more like an apartment than like a hotel. It worked well. Once we found Plaza Florida, I was content for about a year.

Plaza Florida became my new home. The staff really took care of me. They came each day and cleaned my room. They washed any dirty dishes I left. In many ways, they made my transition very easy. They asked my permission if they needed to enter my room to fix something. They warned me when I needed to be aware of something in advance – for example, when they were painting, changing the generator, or washing the windows. It was a great place.

In fact, in many regards it was too great. The Internet worked as long as there was electricity; and really, there weren't very many problems with the electricity. I always had an abundance of hot water. The air conditioning was unbelievable. I absolutely loved to be in my room. When I registered for my room, I asked for two keys, as if my girlfriend were going to stay with me. In reality, it was so I could leave the extra card in the power slot by the door, so the air conditioning would remain on twenty-four-seven. Whenever I left, I would politely turn off the lights; but the electricity card stayed in the slot, and the air conditioning remained on.   Often, when I returned, the shock of the cold air would hit me like a wave.   It was AWESOME!   I could go running, and when I returned to my room it was cold as an icebox.   It was great; at least, I thought so at the time.   Later, I'll talk more about why that may not have been a good idea.

     About a year into my move, I found myself wanting an apartment of my own.   I started looking seriously, spending much time each week seeking out the perfect place.   At about the same time, Plaza Florida had a rate increase.   The fact that they had great service, good electricity, and consistent Internet did not stay a secret for long.   When they raised their prices, it was almost the same cost for me to stay there, as it was to go back to Hotel Santo Domingo.   I actually justified the increase for a few weeks; but one week when I returned, they did not have my room reserved, which made me scramble for a place to stay.   I called several hotels and ended up paying way more than planned to get a room at the Embajador. As a result, I had to start looking again.

     I was upset, because I had been a great client of Plaza Florida for over a year.   I spent more money during that year in their hotel than any other client, yet they lost my reservation.   I was going somewhere else.   If I were not going to earn seniority, I would at least let someone else make money from me.   This time I made several concessions.   I decided I could be a little more flexible with the power and water.   I also made arrangements to use the Internet for several hours each day at Ana's brother's office.

     We found a place called Drake Apart-hotel.   It was clean.   The staff was friendly.   They had a decent breakfast.   And, if I got the room just above the front desk, I had Internet connection. I really buddied up with the workers so they would save this room for me. It got to the point that they knew my schedule and would tell people the room was occupied. That apart-hotel worked out really well for about another year. It cost me around $35 per night. I ended up living there until I moved into my apartment.

I don't know if there is any correlation here or not: but just before I made the move from luxury to more of a normal lifestyle, I had asked my girlfriend to marry me and she had accepted. One of the prerequisites of our situation was that I refused to live in her brother's house when we were married. He had graciously asked me to move in and sleep on the couch until we were married. He is my best friend in the Dominican Republic, and I did not want to upset him, but I had my pride. I was making great money, and was not going to live on a couch, or under a stairway. I was already making sacrifices by living out of a suitcase; I didn't want to move further down the ladder.

In addition to adjusting my living standards, we decided we needed to look at my other expenditures as well. One of my biggest expenses was food. We had made a habit of going to lunch at local restaurants, and then heading out again for dinner. In reality, the cost of doing so was not egregious; but compared to the local Dominican lifestyle, I was overboard. Along with my move from Hotel Santo Domingo to Plaza Florida, we decided to start cooking dinner at home. We figured lunch cost around US$10 for the two of us, so that was not too much (about $60 per week).

One way we reduced expenses was to invite ourselves to Ana's brother's house for lunch every

Wednesday. Our excuse was that I loved *pastalone de plátano maduro*. It is my favorite Dominican food, and Wednesday is the day they made it. The trip to their house is now a tradition (one I am going to keep even when I have kids if possible), and has since saved me every week. We also began going out to dinner only on Friday nights, and other nights we ate in my room at the apart-hotel.

So that we could eat dinners at my place, I actually started to buy food in the local supermarket. I don't know if I really saved money at first because I was buying everything I needed, but the idea was to save money by not spending at restaurants. In reality, the first few weeks, I bought things and then threw them away at the end of the week; or Ana took them to her family. After awhile, I kept two suitcases – one for my clothes and the other for food, or utensils to prepare food. Things like salt, seasonings, can openers, Tabasco, and canned food all add up when you buy them all at once, but if you're going to cook, you need them.

Issues with the Police

As I became more comfortable with living in Santo Domingo, I began to explore more and more. At first I stayed fairly close to my hotel, only investigating a couple of streets away. In fact, my first day of running, I ran around the Hotel Santo Domingo property about ten times. As I became accustomed to living in my new environment, I learned to venture further and further outside of my comfort zone. The most comfortable and logical route was to leave the hotel's property and to run one way or the other down the *Malecon*, which is a main road that runs parallel to the ocean along Santo Domingo's coast. The *Malecon* touches Hotel Santo Domingo's property on one side so it was natural for me to begin my exploring from there.

After I had made it from one end of the *Malecon* to the other, I decided to try to run every road in Central Santo Domingo. I marked out a route on a map and started to expand on it.

In my peak condition, I was running about ten miles a couple of days each week, probably close to 35-40 miles weekly. I would leave Hotel Santo Domingo and run to *Luperon*. At *Luperon*, I would turn right and run up to JFK, where I would once again turn right and head back toward the center of the city. The best I have ever done was one time when, after reaching the center of the city, I continued on to the other side of the river. I actually went to the *Zona Oriental* and returned on the *Malecon,* via the floating bridge. That only happened once. I learned quickly the difference between this side of the river and that side of the river. I haven't been over the river on foot since.

Another thing I began to enjoy was driving. You probably remember that I really like driving and have driven all over the US. Well, after a couple of months in Santo Domingo, always sitting in the passenger seat, I decided it was time to get back in the driver seat. When I began to drive, I was told that the most important rule is not to get in an accident. I guess that really is the only rule. I first started driving Ana's Toyota Corolla. It was a great car, probably something like a 1997. It had about 180,000 miles on it. It had tinted windows, and the tires were terrible. After about a month of getting a flat tire each week, I made Ana get new tires one day. We went to the tire dealer next to Delta (the Toyota dealer) and bought brand-new tires. It was amazing, but the flat tires stopped immediately. I knew the car was not the best vehicle, but it worked, and I had no problems with it once the tires had been changed.

About a year after I began to drive, Ana decided it was a good time for her to get a new vehicle. She decided she would get a *jeepeta*. I was not against the proposition, because there were times when I had driven the Corolla in the rain and I wondered whether it would drown. You have to drive in Santo Domingo to understand what I am talking about here. Cars actually *drown*. They simply take in too much water to continue to live, and they stop dead in their tracks. I had been in situations where I knew we were really close. I had felt the water under my feet as we crept along. Cars are not the right vehicles for Santo Domingo. Small SUVs are much better equipped to deal with the potholes and rain.

When Ana got her new *jeepeta*, I was pretty happy. It had new tires, it would be able to make it through the floods, and generally Ana would be safer. The $45,000 price tag was a different story. In the US, our car was probably worth around $28,000. The problem was that we didn't live in the US. We lived in the Dominican Republic, where the import tax on a vehicle is around 35% of the vehicle's value. In my opinion, we paid almost double what our car was worth; but it worked, so I was happy. Besides, there was nothing I could do about the price tag.

The only problem with the new *jeepeta* was it came "factory". Factory means it came without tinted windows. It had no scratches on it, and it had no metal bumper. It was brand-new. Within a week of getting our new *jeepeta* I started having problems with the police. It was weird, because I had driven in Santo Domingo for just about a year with no problems. I was used to the cars driving the wrong way down the road. I was used to the damn *motos* that came from wherever they come from. I was used to the constant honking. But, for some reason, as a driver of a new *jeepeta* I became a target for the police.

Maybe my driving all of a sudden suffered. Maybe the rules of driving were now suddenly different from the rules of my previous twenty years of driving. Who knows what the difference was? All I know is that in the first two weeks of having a *jeepeta,* I got a ticket for running a red light. In most instances, this is not even an infraction in the Dominican Republic. I also got a ticket for driving without a license plate: not driving without a license, but driving without the license plate. I had the papers from the dealer. I had the temporary plate. I just did not have the actual metal plate.

The AMET, a member of the traffic police agency, said he needed to impound the car. I mean, seriously: how are you supposed to live in a place like this? Luckily my girlfriend, the lawyer, is a sweet talker, so we were able to continue on with just a ticket. It's a ticket with no price, because to this day I have not paid it. Who knows? The day may never come when I feel that ticket is due… Man, I love the Dominican Republic!

Just one week later, I got pulled over again for running a red light. This time I was sure I did not run it. It all happened so quickly at first. My brother-in-law and little sister were visiting. We were driving up *Av. Abraham Lincoln* toward *27 de Febrero*, which are two very busy roads.

We were pulled over by two guys riding a motorcycle. They stopped me, took my license, and then made me go down a side street. Once on the side street, they told me I had committed a major violation and was going to have my car impounded. These were not the normal traffic police (AMET), who wear green. These were members of the *Policia Nacional*, or the National Police, who are responsible for enforcing gun laws and maintaining law and order. National Police wear grey uniforms. In my best Spanish, I told them my wife was an attorney and she worked very nearby. I called her on the phone and told her what was happening. The cop spoke with her for just a second, but quickly hung the phone up. He told me I could not speak on the phone any more. They said I was in serious trouble.

I locked the doors and told my sister, who was sitting in the back of the car, to call Ana and not to hang up, even if she just had to drop the phone on the floor while the line was connected. I did not want to freak them out, so I told them the police were just trying to get a bribe. I started steering the conversation toward a bribe. I told the cop I was willing to pay my fine on the spot if possible, in cash. He seemed to like the idea, but was really looking for more than just a little money. He said he would need to take our car and we could claim it the next day at the main police station. I told him my wife and the policemen who worked at her office would be here in just a minute. If necessary, they would ride with us all to the main police office.

He didn't like the idea of having other visitors. We were in the perfect location for him – about a block off the main road, on the side of a desolate street where few cars passed. We were essentially trapped. I told my sister and her husband we were in no way going to get out of the car; and if he pulled his gun. I was going to try to make a run for it. Keep in mind that the back windows on Toyota RAV 4s are tinted. This meant that the police didn't realize that my sister was talking on the phone in the back seat. She was relaying information to me from Ana. My brother-in-law was sitting shotgun. He had a camera tripod in his lap, which he said would make a great weapon.

I told the policeman my wife was just around the corner. If he wanted to take our fine in cash he had to do it before she got there, because she was really angry. I explained she was coming with three other lawyers, a security guard, and a judge. I don't know why I threw in the judge, but figured it sounded impressive. I said I needed my license back, and I would give him all the cash I had in my wallet. He replied that he wanted only US dollars. I said I had no dollars: if he wanted anything at all, he had about thirty seconds to make a decision. Faster than I care to remember, he grabbed the money I had in my wallet, threw my driver's license into the car, and I hit the gas. I made the end of the street, turned left, and then turned again. I was getting the hell out of there, and fast! We were about two blocks away from Ana's office.

In reality, she was not on her way to rescue me. We only had one car. Her co-workers were also lawyers. They were busy, and there was no way they would have been able to just drop everything and come running. But the policeman didn't know that. My story had worked well. They had been pushed to where they would have had to use severe force, and quickly. They had no idea whether we had weapons or backup. They only knew they had to decide instantly. They figured some *pesos* in their pocket

for sure were better then possibly being able to steal a
jeepeta. I'm just thankful the episode ended so well.

My sister and her husband were laughing about
how we paid the police off. I tried to keep it at that. I
didn't need my family realizing we had almost been car-
jacked. Since then, I have received a ton of great advice
for dealing with the police. I have used it precisely since,
and have had no problems for almost two years.

First, when you are told to pull over, you do not
pull to the side of the road. You make sure you are in the
middle of the busiest part of the street. This serves two
purposes:

1. The police won't want to give you a hard time
   for too long if they're standing in the middle of a
   bunch of cars whose drivers are honking at them;
   and

2. It's going to be difficult to rob you when there are
   bystanders.

One thing is for sure: Dominicans hate corrupt
police. They are likely to jump right into the middle of a
situation, to help out the innocent, or maybe just to get a
piece of the action.

Second, if you are told to pull over, make sure the
cop who's pulling you over has the authority to do so.
The National Police do not have authority to give traffic
tickets. They are something like the National Guard in
the United States. They often set up roadblocks, and stop
cars to look for illegal guns. Due to the dangerous nature
of their work, they most often work in teams. When you
see a National Police roadblock, you know you need to
stop your car. They will be standing on both sides of the
car with M-16s and they will be ready for war. When

you are pulled over in this kind of roadblocks, the group is large enough that it is difficult for them to try to take your money – unless, of course, the whole lot of them are in on the plan!

Third, it is not uncommon for men wearing uniforms like the police to pull people over and to take their cars. This is an easy way for them to car-jack you. They pull you over, then tell you they're impounding your car and you can pick it up tomorrow. One gets inside and drives away, and the other rides off on the *moto*. You are screwed. Stay inside your car!

Finally, being a *gringo* and looking like a rich tourist is a bad thing. You always stand out and will be singled out by predators. At least, that's how it looked to me. I had been selected because I was in a brand-new car, and there were two white guys in the front seat. We were talking and very preoccupied, so we were easy targets.

To counteract the *gringo* image, I decided to get Ana to make her *jeepeta* look really Dominican. We added metal bumpers, both in front and in back. They are ugly, but I figured if I were ever in the same situation again, they would be better if I really did have to run someone over. Besides, most *jeepetas* in the DR have big shiny metal bumpers on the front and the back, so if you touch other vehicles it doesn't hurt your car as much. I also had her put dark tint in the windows. You can see into the car from close by, in the middle of the day; but from a distance it is almost impossible. I always drive with the windows up and the doors locked. I also wear Dominican shades, which are very dark glasses like the cops wore in CHIPS.

Since we put the tint in the windows, I haven't had one single problem with the police. I continue to drive daily. I run red lights just as everyone else does. I drive the wrong way down the road when I need to get right over there. I make illegal left-hand turns. In fact, I drive as much like a local as possible.

I pretty much follow the rules of the road, as I'll teach you in a few pages. Particularly Rule One: don't get hit, at least not too hard. The real police are actually not bad, except when they get involved with directing traffic. They don't make decent wages, and I don't blame them for trying to make a little extra on the side. I am just thankful my family still thinks I bribed the cops…

Buying a House or Apartment

After about a year of hotel life in the Dominican Republic, I began seriously considering buying an apartment. In fact, if I hadn't listened to my girlfriend's advice and eternal caution, I would probably have rented, or bought one, much sooner than that.

I had actually started thinking about buying a house within a few weeks of my first visit. I had gone and looked at apartments without my girlfriend several times. My problem was I was definitely not Dominican. I had problems with the language, the culture, and my tan. You could pick me out of a crowd as a *gringo* from two miles away.

I started my search for an apartment with Ana's blessing about a month after moving into Plaza Florida. I think she expected I would forget about buying after I had seen the prices. She never guessed I was prepared for my visits because I had been scouting around for a while. I had checked out almost every street in the city during my daily runs. The streets I liked I continued to run on, all the time looking for good places for sale. I took pictures of the buildings I liked. If I didn't care for a particular neighborhood, I stopped running there.

When we started looking together, I was really happy. I knew that when Ana was with me, we'd be offered different prices from what I would hear alone.

One of the first places that truly attracted me was in *Mirador Sur*. *Mirador Sur* is an upscale neighborhood close to one of the city's biggest and most popular parks, which sits on a hill with a beautiful view of the ocean. The park is 5 Kilometers in length and several hundred yards wide. It is the perfect place to go running and has many children's play areas, baseball diamonds, walking paths, and more. The Apartment was almost exactly what I would buy if I were buying in the US, as far as amenities and price went. It was about 300 square meters, on the fourth floor of a great building. The apartment had a view of the ocean. The building boasted a pool, excellent parking and security, and – for when the electricity went out – there was *planta full* (its own generator). My only problem with the place was it was $400,000. In the US, I could easily afford the payments on a $400,000 house. Unfortunately, the *Republica Dominicana* required the buyer to pay 18% interest. Unbelievable! In the US, I have a credit score of 800 plus and I make good money. I should be able to afford this place!

The reality was that I could not justify the payment. After considering the interest, mortgage payment, and fees, the apartment would cost close to $5,000 per month US. That was out of my range. After seeing what has happened to the market during the past year, I thank God I didn't try to make it happen with this particular apartment!

During my search, I came upon another terrific apartment. It was close to Ana's office, as well as to the supermarkets. It had a pool. The issue with this place was that the owner wanted to sell it to us without the title.

I know what you're thinking: *"That must have been a typo."* No one would really try to sell a property without owning the title! Actually, they really tried to sell us the property without having clear title. They had purchased the property from an auction where title was supposed to be granted, but at the time we were interested in buying, the title was still unclear. I'm happy we did not push the deal; the property might have been in court for a long time. The title issues might never have been solved – who knows? The lesson I learned here was the value of a good lawyer. Had I not had a lawyer involved in the transaction, I would probably have bought the apartment. And I would never have known for sure whether or not the papers were legitimate.

After longer than I care to admit, we found the perfect place. We are on the third floor of a seven-story building. We have 175 square meters of living space (1600 square feet), with three bedrooms and four bathrooms. There's a service room with living quarters for the household help, and room for washer, dryer, and storage. The breeze from the balcony is absolutely amazing. Our location is very close to downtown Santo Domingo, near my wife's workplace, one of the best malls, several grocery stores, schools, and everything else you could need. It seems very likely to appreciate in value over the next few years. Our apartment will be easy to rent when we decide to upgrade to something bigger. But for now, this place is perfect.

We signed the papers on our home almost exactly

one year before we were able to move in. The process of waiting for the apartment to be completed was very annoying to me. The finish work in the apartment was sub-standard, with many broken tiles, cracks in the walls, and imperfectly sealed doors and windows. In the end, we had to pay someone to come in and re-do the walls. They leveled the doors and re-painted everything, so it looks perfect. The builder promised to repair the floor tile. It has been a year now, and we've just learned to live with the broken tiles. Our guests do not notice them and we don't either, any more.

One of the nicest things about this apartment is that our current house payment is less than what I used to pay for one week at Hotel Santo Domingo. It isn't paid for yet – but one day we'll own it, free and clear.

Getting a Loan from a Dominican Bank

One of the major downsides of the Dominican banking system is the exorbitant interest rates. It is not uncommon to hear of people paying 18% - 20% for their home loans; I have heard of rates as high as 24%. If you have cash, or if you can find a way to finance your property purchase in another country, then do not go with the Dominican loan.

I have researched for months and have never been able to find any way to get a foreign loan to pay for a property in the Dominican Republic. People have written about arranging such favorable foreign loans, and I've called the banks mentioned in the articles; but I never was able to figure it out. I've never met anyone in person who has been able to get a foreign loan on a Dominican property, and neither has anyone I know. I've talked with countless Dominican lawyers about this issue, and no one has any information. As far as I can see, there just is no way to buy a property in the DR with a foreign loan.

It's possible that with very high equity in a US property, you might be able to use that equity to pay for a Dominican Property. I tried this; but by the time I refinanced the first mortgage and added a second mortgage with an interest rate of 12%, it just did not make sense to me.

In order to get a Dominican loan, you have to obtain residency. Once you have become a resident, the loan process is not much different from the loan process in the US. In fact, I think it is a little easier, because the loan officers don't seem to know what they need. In our case, I was able to get a home loan without even showing a check stub. They used my wife's check stub. I had to get a letter from my employer saying that I worked for them (but remember, I was a commission salesman, so there was no guaranteed salary). They checked my US credit and we had the loan.

As I started to become Dominican, I realized the importance of getting a loan in the Dominican Republic, in *pesos*. I have the advantage of making my money in US dollars, which historically are more stable than *pesos*. Another advantage is that the loan is not with a US bank, which means it does not show up on my US credit rating. I have since applied for several lines of credit, and have never even thought of listing the DR loan.

My research has convinced me that it is best to get your loan in Dominican *pesos* because it is tied to the market where you will be living. The loan will also be easier to pay if you are earning in *pesos*. If you are paid in dollars, you can easily change the dollars to *pesos* to make your payments. I think we have done pretty well on our apartment, despite our interest rate being 16%.

Let me explain how I view a typical real estate deal in the Dominican Republic. A decent two to three bed-room apartment in Santo Domingo's nicer neighborhoods will run between RD$5,000,000 and RD$7,000,000. When I was first looking for apartments the exchange rate was 32.5 Pesos to 1 US Dollar. At that time the apartments were running between US$153,000 and US$200,000. Apartments also are often purchased much before they are completed, with entire buildings being sold out prior to any occupancy. We bought an apartment in a building still under construction. It was about 90% completed when we bought.

By the time we closed on the apartment, the exchange rate was 34 to 1; and at the time of the writing of this book, the exchange rate is 36 to 1. Due to the deflation of the *peso* vs. the US dollar, a typical apartment now would cost between US$139,000, and US$194,000. Now, don't think this means that the apartments are worth less now just because the exchange rate has changed. Not at all! Most apartments have appreciated, are now selling for somewhere in the neighborhood of RD$6,200,000, to RD$8,000,000 (or US$174,000 to US$220,000) at the current exchange rate. When the exchange rate is good, Ana and I exchange money to pay on our house. I hope the *peso* does not devalue much more than it has so far; continued devaluation would cause a lot of inflation in consumer goods, which I think are already too expensive.

Based on my research, I believe the *peso* will stay in the 34-to-35 range. This is probably the best range for everyone. I have read about a time when it went as far down as 50-to-1. Some homeowners made a killing. I also know the *peso* has been as high as 15-to-1. If that were to happen, we would no longer exchange dollars for *pesos*. We would simply make the payments out of my wife's check. We're hedging our investment by using dollars to pay when the exchange rate is high; but if it ever goes down, we are protecting ourselves with Ana's income. It has worked out really well so far.

Exchanging Money

During my first few years in the DR, I withdrew money from the ATM each week when I was in Santo Domingo. I figured it was safer than exchanging money on the street, and I got pretty good rates from my bank. This, however, was not a good long-term option. The problem was that the Dominican ATMs would only let me withdraw a small amount each day. In the long run this was not a good way to live—withdrawing money day after day to save for a weekend get away, or other larger purchase. If I had remained reliant on the Dominican ATMs and their ridiculously low limits it would simply take way too long to get any substantial amount of money.

As a result, I decided to try to withdraw any cash money I needed while I was in the US and then just bring the cash home with me. (And by now, "home" for me was the DR.) I bought a money belt and arranged with my bank to let me withdraw more than the normal daily limit. If I needed money any particular week I would go to the bank and withdraw the maximum allowed per transaction. If I needed more, I would continue to make withdrawals until I had what I needed. Now, I knew I was not allowed to carry more than $10,000 at a time while traveling internationally, but I was actually more worried about being robbed than I was about getting questioned by the government about having a couple grand with me. To try to make it less likely to lose all of the money were I robbed I would always split up the money and carry it in different pockets and the money belt, which I wore inside my pants.

I remember one trip where I had several thousand dollars in cash, and I had to take a taxi from the airport to my hotel. I was nervous, but the taxi driver had no idea about the money, so I figured I was safe. After arriving in Santo Domingo, I would either have it deposited into a US-dollar account or we would have a moneychanger meet us at the bank, where we would exchange dollars for pesos.

One time when we were changing dollars to pesos, I noticed that the representative of the exchange company arrived to the bank on a *moto*, wearing a small backpack. He looked just like any other guy on a *moto*. He confidently walked up to the counter and took off his backpack. When he opened it up, I noticed it was literally full of cash! First he deposited the equivalent of about US$50,000 in his company's account. He then made the transaction with us. He gave the cashier our money; she counted it and deposited it into our account. We gave him the US money. He put it in his backpack, which was now much less full. While we were talking with this man at the bank, he told us that he once had to kill a guy for trying to take his backpack.

What I usually carried with me was peanuts compared to what this guy had on a daily basis, but I am happier not dealing with that amount of stress. I worried too much any time I had any amount of cash with me. Since hearing that story I have always made much smaller exchanges. To me it seems like there's less chance of being robbed or getting shot. We get a little lower on the exchange but to me it is worth not stressing about losing a lot of money, or worse getting killed. I prefer to be safe. Period.

Dealing with Window Washers

The first time you visit the Dominican Republic, you'll be amazed by the nice young men who vigilantly stand by the stop signals, just to wash your windshield. It will amaze you to see them sweating while they work so hard to wash every bug off. They will rub your windshield so vigorously that you'll think they are trying to rub a hole in it.

Your second visit, you'll think they are amusing; but it will seem a bit excessive to get your windows done at every stoplight. By the third visit, you'll learn they are not really washing your windshield. That stuff on the rag they are using or in the bottle they spray from is not even clean water. It is really sticky and dirty, and will make not just your window but also your whole car dirtier. When you get to the DR for your fourth visit, you'll be on the lookout for those sneaky buggers who come up from behind and throw their wet rag on your window. You will learn quickly to wave your forefinger back and forth, while yelling "NO! NO! NO! NO!" at the top of your lungs so they can hear you well through your rolled-up windows.

You will learn to be heartless. You'll expect to hear, "Give me a hundred, and if you don't have that, give me whatever you've got." You'll realize that they call you dirty names and say even worse things to your wife. You'll learn they are just like rats – out to take, and take, and take. You'll learn they really do sneak. They are vermin.

One of my main strategies with these guys is to try to act tough. I have seen them swarm over the cars of women and people who look unlikely to argue with them, but they skip the car of the man who looks tough. The guy in the new Jeep or the Mercedes who wears dark shades is passed over entirely. The guy who obviously has cash, but who looks hard and is possibly carrying a weapon is not even considered. These men are ignored because they would just as soon get out of the car and beat the "helpers" up as sit in the car and tell them no. The window washers leave the tough guy alone.

I try to turn into that guy when I get to the stoplights. I sit looking straight ahead. My dark shades are on, and my head keeps the rhythm of the loud music on my radio. When the window washers look at my car, I look them directly in the eye, very quickly, and only once. If they move even a millimeter toward my car, I shake my head "no". It's clear by my expression that I'm saying, "Don't even *think* about touching my car! I don't want a window wash, and you do *not* want to make me tell you so." I give them respect, but at the same time exude confidence. They see that guy and pass on to the next prospective customer.

Every now and then, they catch me when I'm not on guard. They sneak up like a fox from behind. They come out from behind a bush, or slink out from behind a truck, when I'm not paying attention. They slide out of nowhere when I am buying a phone card. It seems as if I buy a phone card and get that dirty rag on my front window almost every time at the same stop. Recently I've been telling the man who sells phone cards, "If that guy touches my car with his dirty rag, I'm buying the phone card from someone else."

About every three months, I get caught like this. I begin by saying, "NO!" Then I say, "Fine, go ahead, but I'm not going to pay you anything. The guy behind me wants to have his windows done." I just have to go back immediately to being that tough guy – and they go away. As soon as they are not in power, they go. If they succeed and get into the wash before I can stop them, I'll give them a couple of *pesos;* but that doesn't happen very often.

Now, I have seen window washers throw rocks and bricks at cars. I have seen them hit cars and threaten drivers. The trick is to be The Guy: the one they don't know how to read. Are you a tough guy packing heat? Are you going to get out and put that washer someplace uncomfortable? Are you going to do something else? Mystery is your friend. Usually a quick shake of the head and a "No!" will get the point across. Clear confidence that you will not put up with them is the main point. Remain confident. but don't act like an ass, and you'll win!

People Who Think I Will Give Them Stuff

As I said earlier, Ana taught me from the start not to give anything to anyone. I have done pretty well at this. One exception was after we had moved into our new apartment. Our building is a new seven-story tower, with a total of 21 apartments. As in most buildings, we have a gentleman who lives there and is responsible for taking care of the building. He mops the tile floors. He meets you at the door and takes out the trash for you. He'll help when you have too many groceries to carry up on your own, and in many other situations. Every once in a while he washes our car. He's there in the morning to open the gate, and he's there at night to make sure everything is safe. He is a great guy.

Soon after we moved in, I noticed that he had a DVD player and really enjoyed watching movies. One day my wife told me his DVD player had broken and he was pretty upset. It was probably the most expensive asset he owned. These watchmen, or guardians, are often Haitian immigrants who live on the premises and are paid very low wages. They have few belongings; and for our guardian to have a DVD player was pretty cool for him. He not only watched movies alone, but would have friends over to socialize. Many other watchmen and workers from neighboring buildings would come by and hang out and watch movies with him. Listening to music and watching movies was a big part of his life.

After I heard that his DVD player had broken, I noticed he was very down. I felt bad for him because I knew he wouldn't be able to buy another one for a long time. I don't know what his wages are, but I am sure it would take him a year or more to save up enough to get a replacement. I told my wife we should give him the portable DVD player we had. I had one I had used for a year or so when I traveled. She had used it to watch movies a few times; but usually the thing just sat in our closet. We didn't use it, since there was a DVD player attached to our television. We really didn't need it. This poor guy was sitting downstairs, alone, away from his family, and now with a major part of his social life gone. I really felt badly for him.

Ana warned me that if we gave him a DVD player, he would tell other people. We would become "the rich people". She was particularly worried that if I gave it to him, I would be considered a rich *gringo* dude who would give anyone anything. I told her she should probably be the one to give it to him, because he knew she was Dominican. He knew she wouldn't just give her other things away for no reason. He would also respect the fact that I did not want to get involved. Well, as it turned out, Ana was right and I was wrong.

About four months after we gave our watchman the DVD player, the screen went out. He first complained to my wife. He then complained to me. Ana said, "Well, it's yours; if you want it fixed, you need to get it fixed." Once again, I felt bad. Those things cost about $100 in the US.

I worry that people think I am wealthy, but I also do a pretty good job of hiding the amount of money I make. When the watchman asked my assistance for the DVD player, he asked as if he thought I could fix it myself. I took a look at it, and was able to tell the mechanical parts worked fine. It was the screen that was broken. I examined it for about five minutes. I had no idea what I was doing. I suggested that maybe he could have the screen replaced. I told him I would "ask my friend" the next time I went to the US, but I didn't know how much it would cost him.

That seemed to be fine with him. The next day the machine was working perfectly. Now, what really happened? Did the machine magically fix itself? Did he figure out how to make the screen work? Was he trying to put one over on me? I really don't know. He told me he had taken it to a shop and for about $25 they had

changed the screen. Who knows? I don't, nor do I care
to find out. I think he was telling me the truth; but part of
me feels like a sucker. I still wonder – but I also learned
a lesson.

The lesson was really not even part of that story.
The lesson came from the superintendent of our building.
This man sits downstairs and is apparently responsible
for making sure things go perfectly in our building. I'm
not exactly certain what he does, but he sits with his
feet up on the chair in front of him. Usually, his head
is propped back against the building. Many times when
I go downstairs, his eyes are closed and he pretends he
can't hear me. I always say "Hi." Not many people
would be rude enough not even to answer, so maybe he's
really sleeping. If so, he sleeps for about five hours each
day. He wakes up long enough to yell at the guy who
lives there, and to smoke a cigarette; and then he goes
back to sleep. Around 2:00, he wakes up and eats lunch.
After lunch he takes a quick two-hour nap before heading
home. What a life!

One day, not long after I had given the guard the
DVD player, this superintendent stopped me when I
returned from running. (Keep in mind that I'm the guy
who cannot speak Spanish.) He announced that he really
needed a radio. The one he had was useless when he
walked through the building, he said, because it had to be
plugged into an outlet. He needed a small one he could
carry in his shirt pocket. I thought, "Dude, you just sit
there listening to the radio all day, and you sleep most
of the afternoon. I have *never* seen you walking through
the building!"

He explained that he needed two things from me:
the cordless radio and some running shoes. He needed

running shoes just like the ones I had on. In fact, he said, he wore the same size I did. How would he know that? He's about a foot taller than I am, and has at least a hundred pounds on me. I doubt very much we wear the same size shoe. I thought, "You're sitting here in front of my house and telling me you need me to go buy you things..? I can't believe it!"

I said, "Well, I really don't have other running shoes, and I surely don't have a radio." His reply astonished me. "That's all right," he said. "You can buy me a radio the next time you're in the US. And don't worry about the running shoes – I'll just take these that you're wearing, because I know you have more than one pair."

What? This guy had the nerve to tell me I had more than one pair of shoes, so I should give one pair to him! I was just about ready to blow up at him when I remembered something. He really didn't know anything about me. I told him I would look and see what I had in the house. I also made it a point to wear only those same running shoes when he was there. I told him I'd look the next time I was in the States.

During the next couple of months, I continued to look for his radio. I never found it. I also tried to find his running shoes. They never appeared either. My problem was that this guy thought I was just going to give in to his demands. Remember the lesson about how many poor Dominicans will think you owe them something if you have more money than they do? This is the perfect example. I kept telling him I was looking, until my Spanish was good enough to inform him that I was not going to look any more. I told him I didn't have enough money even to think about buying him something. I said I'd be happy to give him my old shoes when I was done with them. He agreed. That was that.

The lesson was: Never give a DVD player to someone for no reason. I'll probably always be marked as the stupid white guy who gave the watchman a DVD player. Never again!

How to Honk a Horn Properly

The first time you drive in the Dominican Republic, you will go through the several stages of excitement, fear, and sudden almost uncontrollable anger. The excitement begins as soon as you realize you are driving on streets with lights, lane lines, and signs that look similar to those in the US; but you're sharing those streets with drivers and their vehicles that don't drive, or act, anything like the drivers and vehicles you are used to.

Driving and the rules of the road in the DR will be discussed a little later in the book. Here, I only want to write about honking and the lessons I have learned. In the US, I have driven for years without hearing a horn honk. In most of the Western United States, it is considered rude if you pull up in front of someone's house and honk to let them know you are there. It is *very* rude if you honk when a light turns green and the car in front of you does not immediately move. You would probably get run off the road if you honked as you passed someone on the freeway, especially if you were just honking to let them know you were there.

These traditional rules of driving courtesy should be forgotten as soon as you put the key in the ignition of your Dominican vehicle. In the Dominican Republic, the only requirement for a vehicle to be considered roadworthy is a functional horn. There are no other environmental or safety requirements. Use of a vehicle's horn is as necessary as using the steering wheel, brakes, and accelerator. Honking is not considered rude. In fact, you are expected to honk; and it is often considered rude if you *don't* honk to let someone know you are there. It is good to give the other drivers a friendly signal, just in case they weren't paying attention and did not notice you were in the vicinity. You have to think of it as a "courtesy honk". They will appreciate it. In turn, you will be given many courtesy honks from the other considerate drivers.

As you enter your vehicle before your first driving experience in the DR, the first thing you need to do is honk the horn. It does not matter where you're sitting: just honk it. Make sure it works. If it does not work, do not drive the vehicle. You are certain to run into a situation where you will be forced to stop, due to your inability to navigate without the horn. As long as the horn is in proper functioning order, you are ready for your first Dominican driving experience.

Now, as you begin to drive for the first time, the proper way to hold the wheel is with one hand on the wheel and the other on the horn. You will surely need both hands. They will both be busy, so don't think for a second you will be able to do anything else with either hand. One hand will maneuver the vehicle, control the turn signals, change the radio station, and roll the windows up and down. The other hand will operate the horn. The rules for honking are as follows:

<u>Honk One</u>: <u>Honk any time you feel that another vehicle (car, *moto*, horse, bike, truck, cart, unidentifiable vehicle, or combination of any of the above vehicles) needs to know you are there.</u> This first honk is usually

performed to tell them you are going to pass them, so they
need to move over just a little. The proper honk to use
in this situation is a short *bep-bep* honk. Nothing long,
nothing drastic. Just let them know you're there, possibly
in their blind spot, and you're going to be passing. You
need to use this honk so they know not to come into your
lane as you pass – because no one uses a blinker. This
honk is your proactive way to tell them not to come into
your lane.

As you begin to drive, you will quickly notice
that the lane lines designating parallel spaces to contain
vehicles in most other parts of the world are not used for
that purpose here. Lane lines in the Dominican Republic
represent nothing but lines painted on the road. They are
not to be considered similar in any way to lines you may
be used to seeing in any other country. Drivers can drive
between them, use them as a guide for the center of their
vehicle, or ignore them entirely.

Honk Two: Start to honk as soon as the signal light
turns green. This second type of honk serves two purposes:
to tell the people in front of you to go, and to make sure
any cars crossing or continuing through the red light know
you are going to enter the intersection. The proper honk to
use in this situation is just a little longer then the previous
honk. It is a serious safety issue to be hit broadside by a
vehicle whose driver thinks it is still safe to go through the
intersection, even on a red light. The warning honk will
let them know you plan to take advantage of your green
light, and are about to enter the intersection. *Beep. Beep.*
Again, nothing drastic is needed.

It is considered very polite to let all the drivers
in front of you, as well as those who intend to continue
through the intersection despite the red light in front

of them, know you plan on entering the intersection. Those drivers in front of you often are preoccupied, and appreciate your letting them know it is time to go. The drivers crossing from the other directions also appreciate knowing if you want to go. If you fail to let them know you're going to enter the intersection, you'll likely need to sit and wait for the other drivers to decide what *they* are going to do.

Honk Three: <u>Honk when you see a vehicle ahead that is about to turn in front of you.</u> This third honk is used whenever you need to continue in the direction you are going, but you see another vehicle that may block your path. If you see a car or *moto* parked perpendicular to the road, and you think its driver may either try to cross or turn in front of you, this honk is a must. It will enable you to move on to one of the more aggressive honks discussed below without being a jerk, so make sure you use it. It is just barely longer than Honk Number Two: *Beeep. Beeep.*

This is partly a safety honk and partly a warning honk — nothing threatening. It is a friendly warning that you are on the road headed in their direction, and do not plan to stop between where you are and where they are. Often people here do not know exactly whether you plan to continue in the same direction or make a sudden stop or turn. If they misread your plans they may just decide you are going to stop suddenly; so they will feel it is fine to go ahead and cross, or pull in front of you. Use Honk Number Three, and then you'll be able to use Honks Number Four and Five without being the bad guy. Honk Three is the last of the warning honks. From here, the honks get much more aggressive, and are necessary to defend your rights proactively.

Honk Four: <u>You are obligated to honk whenever the *Autoridad Metropolitana de Transporte* (AMET) holds you up for longer than a minute or two</u>. The proper time to honk is when you see the light turn green for the second time after the AMET stopped traffic. If they stop the traffic in the direction you are going, don't honk when the light turns green the first time. Remember, they are taking care of important police business and need to make sure traffic flows well throughout the city. If the AMET agent stopped your direction of traffic, and then loses track of time while talking with a friend or other driver, and he forgets to let your direction of traffic start again, it is proper to remind him you are waiting there when the light turns green for the second time.

Most of the cars will start with Honk Number One. (A reminder for beginners: Number One is just a friendly warning honk – *bep bep.*) After reminding the AMET that you're waiting and the light has changed several ti-mes since he stopped traffic, you need to move on to Honk Number Two. This will provide a little stronger reminder: *beep beep.* If nothing happens, it's time to move on to Honk Three and give the longer, but still friendly, warning/reminder honk—*Beeep Beeep.* If Number Three doesn't do the job, move on to Honk Number Four.

This honk is the "it is our turn" honk. This honk is just below the level of an aggressive honk. It's a more sustained (and, hopefully, more annoying) honk designed to get the AMET to let you go: *BEEeep BEEeep BEEeep BEEeep.* Some drivers skip this step. However, I highly recommend it, because it often does the trick. Use it sparingly – if you are the only person honking, this one tends to annoy other drivers, as well. Honk Four works best in unison with other drivers. It is most effective when

40-50 cars join in the task together. You'll probably only get to use this honk once or twice a week, so enjoy the chance while it lasts.

<u>Honk Five</u>: Honk Number Five is used on those special occasions when you just get to the end of your rope with the horrendous drivers in the Dominican Republic. Always remember that Honk Five can cause other drivers to become combative. Also, before you decide to use Honk Number Five, remember that many Dominicans carry guns. Honk Five is an aggressive and ceaseless honk; while you're honking, you also need to wave your free hand and yell. You simply lean on the horn and don't let up until you get what you want.

Some idiot has completely blocked four lanes of traffic because he stopped in the middle of the inter-section? Perfect! Use Honk Number Five. The AMET has refused to remember that your lane of traffic has been passed over for three or four green lights? No problem: Honk Five. Someone decided to turn left from the right lane, and stopped in front of all the traffic, waiting for the cross-light to turn red and his light to turn green? You know it – Honk Five.

Honk Five can be taken to the next level by rolling down your window and yelling out the window at the offender (if your Spanish is good enough and you look tough). This can also be accomplished with a wave. There is a special wave that is universal, and consists of waving the back of your hand at the offending party with all the fingers in a fist, with the exception of the middle one, which remains at full salute. I have never used this wave because I have never really wanted to see the front end of a gun. This wave, coupled with Honk Number Five, should be used extremely sparingly. It should be kept for the most dire situations.

Honking usually starts with Honk Number One; you work your way up to Honk Number Five, as the situation requires. Learn to honk properly: you'll find it refreshing to greet other drivers and let them know you are there. Dominican drivers are actually very courteous, and will return the favor. It's rather nice to know you can count on their informing you when they are planning to pass. I like it. At first, I used to set a minimum honk requirement for myself, to become accustomed to using the horn when I was driving along. Ana also told me when to use the horn; she sometimes insisted I was a dangerous driver because I didn't use the horn enough. Once I learned to use the horn the way the Dominicans do, it was safe for me to drive anywhere in the country. After almost four years driving in the Dominican Republic, I am Dominican enough. I just use the horn as needed. Don't worry about driving; it's not that tough… as long as you don't let the honking get under your skin!

Spanish Classes

About two months after my first visit to the DR, I decided to enroll in Spanish classes. I figured it was probably smart to just go ahead and learn Spanish even if I didn't end up living in the Dominican Republic. My first Spanish classes taught me many of the basic necessities:

- Hi! (*¡Hola!*)
- How are you? (*¿Cómo tu 'tá?*)
- I am hungry. (*Tengo hambre.*)
- I am tired. (*Tengo sueño.*)
- Where are the bathrooms? (*¿Dónde están los baños?*)

I learned a few new phrases, but mostly just the basics. I learned these things in the first couple of classes, and then stupidly decided it was probably better to learn Spanish on my own. (Besides, at the time, I still thought I'd be able to talk this Dominican girl into moving to the US.)

For about a year, I did nothing about formal Spanish classes. What changed my mind was the day that two men dressed like policemen tried to take my car, and almost succeeded. It wasn't until then that it hit me that I was living in a country where I could understand hardly anything. I decided if I was going to continue living in Santo Domingo, I needed to get serious about learning Spanish. I found a private tutor and began my classes.

Over the next months, my Spanish progressed from basic to intermediate. I was able to understand about half of all conversations, and I felt I could explain myself if I needed to. I could tell the taxi driver where to go. I could call the *Colmado* (the local market) and order water, Coke™, and other simple things. I felt I was fine.

I learned the future tense of some verbs, some past tense, and present tense. It was really just more of the basics. I couldn't get by in a group. I could not take a whole conversation on in Spanish. I couldn't really live without Ana holding my hand; but I made it. This is one of my greatest regrets: I should have continued the classes, and I should have become fluent sooner. I should have become totally Dominican by learning their language.

I believe a person can go from zero Spanish to basic Spanish in a matter of a few weeks of practice. From there, a person can advance to intermediate Spanish over a period of about two to three intensive months of practice. To become entirely fluent probably will take a year, but it is time and effort very well spent.

Understanding Spanish has enabled me to comprehend
what's going on around me. It has helped me at work,
as well as in my personal life. I now am able to talk to a
whole new group of people at airports and around town.
I am able to have conversations with my wife's family
and friends. It is something I should have gotten serious
about a long time ago.

The Stress of Leaving Everything Behind

I read an article once about entering into a
relationship where one party had to give up more than the
other. The article noted that there was a tendency for the
second person to feel some level of guilt, because they felt
responsible for the first person's sacrifices. I have made it
a point never to talk about missing my family. I make sure
I don't compare the amount of time I get with my family
with the amount of time my wife gets with her family.
That would not be fair. I try to let her know I am happy to
be here, and I don't allow our conversations ever to reach
the point where she feels any guilt for my sacrifices.

With that said, one of the most stressful things
for me to deal with has been the lack of my own friends
and family. All our friends are really Ana's family and
friends, who have befriended me because of her. All my
family is really my wife's family, who has adopted me.
I know they are her friends first and my friends second,
and that's fine with me.

My issues have come when my family has had
reunions, or had time together for a holiday or birthday,
and I've missed out. At times this causes me stress,
because I give up events I have enjoyed my whole life.
Sometimes I've even felt that my wife should have been

more understanding. Nonetheless, I've tried not feel that my sacrifices are her fault.

I am able to maintain friendships and keep relationships with my family strong by talking on the phone with them. I also try to visit at least one family member each quarter. I would rather see them for a few days several times each year than ten days all at once. It seems this also allows me to keep a closer relationship. It has also enabled me to make a personal visit on one end or the other of a business trip. I pay a small amount and change a ticket so I can stay a day or two with a family member. I have done this all over the country, and it has actually worked out very well.

Some of the harder times for me are the US holidays, like the Fourth of July. The Dominican Republic does not celebrate this holiday, so my wife has to work. I have almost nothing to do, and it is not really fun to celebrate alone, so I usually act as if it were just another day. There is no Thanksgiving here, Halloween is different, Christmas is not nearly the same as in the US, and the reality is that more of the Dominican holidays are different than similar. The holiday I miss the most is the Fourth of July. Every year on the Fourth I find myself thinking about barbecues, watermelon, and fireworks, as well as the feeling of family on a day that's important to most Americans.

I have made it a point to try to visit my family during the winter holidays each year. I think Christmas is a time to see family; I feel that my visit then has been well worth the time and money spent. I have also tried to spend a few days each summer with my family. I haven't made the Fourth yet, but this year I've got it marked on the calendar.

...issing family, I miss many American ...s. I miss having friends just drop by ...l Sunday afternoon to watch football. ...ot use television as a pastime when they ...Dominicans keep most television sets ...lroom, because they feel it is distracting, and makes ...versation difficult. I prefer to sit on the couch, watching a football game with my friends and eating freshly cooked meat.

When I lived in the US, I spent several days fishing each month on a lake or river close to my house. In the fall, I would hunt deer and elk. In the winter, I would hunt pheasants and geese. These pastimes are gone. I don't know why I do not hear of more Dominicans fishing, but the only fishing I have seen is a few guys down on the *Malecon* trying to catch some small bottom-feeders. There is no such thing as hunting in the DR. I guess I'll just have to chalk that up to past experience and move on.

I have been able to maintain my running, and even take it to a whole new level. Since I moved to Santo Domingo, I have logged thousands of miles of running. I have run on every major road, most small roads, and a lot of the ones that are not really even roads. I run near the ocean. I run through the park. My new pastime is running. It is something I can do almost every day of the year. My running allows me time on my own, in my own world. I can run fast when I want and walk when I want. I can go near the water and feel the spray. I can run down back alleys, and see living conditions and sights I have never seen before. I can head to the park and listen and watch the parrots. During the right times of year, I can find fresh mangos, ready to eat. I am always able to run in shorts and a sleeveless shirt. I never have to wear long

pants when I go run. I guess that's neither good n
it's just different. When you leave some pastimes l
you also gain a lot of new experiences. I have
embrace the good in the new and forget about the past.
What I have left, I remember as my personal treasures.
The life and all of the wonderful memories I have gained
in the Dominican Republic are my new riches. I look
forward to all the new and exciting surprises I will
continue to discover about this life and this experience.
¡Viva la Republica Dominicana!

Internet Issues

In this book, I am attempting to paint a fair picture
of life in the Dominican Republic. I try to put life in the
right perspective. I am not trying to paint a picture of
a luxurious life with a maid and cook. I am purposely
not painting the picture so that people think life here is
just beautiful babes on the beach, sipping margaritas and
enjoying the sun. I am painting as realistic a picture as
possible, from my own perspective. I'm not trying to
gloss over the things that truly cause me pain, worry,
or anguish. I'm not trying to oversell the wonderful
fruits and vegetables – although really, the avocados and
mangos alone are enough to make a person move to the
Dominican Republic!

I also need to be very clear that I live a lifestyle that
is more extravagant than that of the normal Dominican
family. Our building has a twenty-four-hour back-up
generator. We have a big underground tank of water in
case of emergencies. I have "high speed" Internet. So
from the perspective of many Dominicans, I actually
have it easy.

Now, let me get into a few of the problems with the infrastructure that absolutely drive me wacky. It simply amazes me to go somewhere and find there is no power. I even sometimes laugh right out loud when I go into a store and the lights are out, yet it is just "business as usual". People walk around as if nothing is different from when those fixtures hanging from the ceiling actually produce light. It baffles me!

I am just Internet-savvy enough to know you need to plug a wire in the wall and then plug the other end into a router for the Internet to be floating in the air all around you. I also am sufficiently electrically inclined to know that the little router box needs power. It makes sense that the little green lights on the front of it go dark when there is no power. That's how everything works, right? Well, in the Dominican Republic, the Internet works, or maybe I should say "operates", a little differently from elsewhere.

First of all, the power issues I mentioned above wreak havoc on the poor little routers. Like most small electronics, they just do not like it when the power flickers here or there. It seems they can only run at full power; they don't know anything else. Because we have a twenty-four-hour generator, when the power goes out in our section of the city, our generator will turn on and give us power. It ought to work like a charm. If you live without a generator, you either have a back-up battery system or you go without power completely for hours and hours on end. In the longer power outages, the batteries die; and with no generator and no batteries, you just do without power completely until your area of the city has electricity again. If you have a generator, you're good to go – at least until you run out of Diesel.

Now, generators run on motors, which need a little time to warm up and start producing electricity. This means that you have a lag time: your power goes off, but in less than a minute it will come back on. The problem is that the little router thing also goes off when the power stops. Then when the generator kicks on, the router needs some time to reboot; so you have a three- to four-minute break from whatever you are doing. From some perspectives, it may be nice to have a much-needed break several times a day. But if you are on a phone call, you also get a break from talking. If you are sending an email, you get a break from whatever you had written. If you are chatting with a friend on MSN, you simply *disappear* off the face of the earth when the power goes out. It's as if the entire world has to work around the Dominican Republic's power issues.

To combat this constant nuisance of not being able to function like a human in the modern world, I decided to buy a back-up battery. In the US, you can actually get batteries to save your computer from power outages. They give you up to fifteen minutes to close everything and turn off your computer. Perfect! My little router thing turns off, and then is back up in three or four minutes; so one of these little back-up batteries should work perfectly. Right? I would bet that in almost every place on the planet, that would be a great idea. Here, it fixes the power problem. I guess our Internet provider found out I had actually figured a way to get Internet access solidly, throughout the day and night – so they decided to give us intermittent Internet outages.

This is the second, and in my current view, the far worse problem. The Internet companies charge you for a certain speed of Internet. If you want fast Internet, you pay a lot; but if you are an Internet addict like me—IT IS WORTH IT! The Internet companies then decide you should not really be given the speed you are paying for; so they put limits on the speed at which you can upload and download. They do it with no particular reason and at no designated time, so you *cannot* plan ahead. They simply decide you are going to have dial-up speed – and BAM! The Internet is gone. The trick is to call them and complain. Normally, you'd figure, you call and they fix it. This is true – except they will only fix it while you are calling! By the next day, it will be gone again. Call, and they fix it. The next day, call again.

Here's the way it goes: Call. Wait on hold. Get the technician on the phone; he reads a list of questions to try to "help you troubleshoot your problem", as if you hadn't already tried all those ideas. When you are done with the list, they check your line on their end and say "Yeah, it does seem slow. Let me try something. Did that fix it?" Magically, the Internet is back. The next day the same thing happens. And it's just like the movie "Groundhog Day" – but this time it's with a twenty-year-old Dominican kid on the other end of the phone, who has never used a computer for anything except for checking out Myspace and porn.

I have decided that if I am going to suffer, then my Internet provider will suffer too. So my new trick is to tell them the Internet is not working. When they fix it, I say it still seems not to be working, and they need to send out a technician. The technicians have been here many times. Each time, they look at the speed on my computer and say it is working. I simply respond, "I guess it must be working right now, but most of the time it doesn't work."

This strategy probably won't fix my problem; but

at least I get a little satisfaction out of knowing I am giving them a pain in the neck just like the one I have. I am very courteous. I thank them so much for coming to my house. I also tell the technician I am going to continue to call and make them come out until they get me the speed I am paying for.

This last time, it actually worked. I haven't had the Internet cycling for about a week, and the speed has almost been fast. I think the plan is working. Unfortunately, this is the only one of my major issues from which I've been able to get any sort of revenge or satisfaction. Other problems, I'll just have to chalk up to the joys of the Dominican Lifestyle.

One last thought. If you move to an area that is out of the city or does not have twenty-four-hour electricity, you'll be in for a big shock. The issues I have just complained about are nothing, compared to what you will have to deal with. Just get ready to smile, light a candle, and grab a cold drink from the fridge while it is still cool.

Traffic

I have been driving for more than twenty years. In that time, I have learned a little about how to control a vehicle and the rules of the road. To begin with, I grew up in Southern California, where rush hour lasts from 6AM to 10AM and from 4PM to 7PM. I have driven in New York City with the world's most notoriously aggressive taxi drivers. I have conquered New Jersey and its hard-nosed delivery trucks. I have driven all over the country, both for work and pleasure, from North to South and from East to West. I have pulled trailers all over the country, transported boats for hundreds of miles, and towed cars that have broken down. I have driven on roads so icy and snow-covered the Department of Transportation closed them. I have driven in mud, through the desert, over mountains, and offroad. I have driven in Australia, where they drive on the wrong side of the street. I have driven in Malaysia where they have no rules for following too closely. In Canada, driving is just about like in the US, except they use kilometers instead of miles. I have been in accidents and seen tragic driving situations where many were injured. However, nothing has prepared me for the horrendous driving conditions I endure on a daily basis when driving in the Dominican Republic.

One of the first things you'll be asked by a Dominican who lives in the United States is whether you drive. It is almost as if they're testing you to see if you are either brave or stupid. Driving is something I have done forever. I like the ability to go where I want when I want. Living in the Dominican Republic has not changed that. I learned very quickly that the drivers are aggressive. The roads are not maintained. The *motos* are so daring you have to assume there is always one in each blind spot.

When I first visited the DR, my girlfriend drove everywhere. She thought the driving in the DR was more difficult than elsewhere, so she would not allow me to drive. After a few visits I was allowed to take a shot at driving. At first I felt it was no big deal, but I soon changed my mind. In my opinion, the fact that cars go whichever way they want on a road is no big deal. You get used to looking for some idiot who needs to go *right over there*, so he drives the wrong way down a one-way street. It is normal to see a person who missed a turn just stop and back up, even if it is a major and busy road. No problem. The *moto* drivers are so uneducated they drive over curbs, down the sidewalks, and weave in and out of traffic. I saw a statistic once that showed something like "seven out of every one thousand *moto* drivers die each year, and fifty out of every thousand are seriously injured." The driving is such a nightmare because, in my opinion, most people should not be entitled to drive.

If you are going to move to the DR permanently you'll have to get used to driving sooner or later. Here are the rules as I see them:

Rule #1 – Do not get hit, at least not too hard.
Rule #2 – Do not hit anyone else, at least not too hard.
Rule #3 – If you see an AMET (the traffic police), act as if you are obeying normal traffic laws.
Rule #4 – Plan to take an extra thirty minutes to get wherever you're going, because traffic is unpredictable.
Rule #5 – If you look like a *gringo*, you are probably going to get some tickets.

Let me explain each rule in a little more detail.

<u>Rule #1 – Do not get hit, at least not too hard.</u>
The reality is that you are going to get hit. There are just no two ways about it. I have been rear-ended five times, each time by some dude who was just not paying attention. You get a couple of scratches on your car, but life goes on. To protect yourself and your car, you need to add those ugly metal bumpers you see on all the cars –

front and rear. Problem solved. Obey rule one and you'll
live longer.

Rule #2 – Don't hit anyone else, at least not too
hard. It is a good general rule not to cause damage to
someone else's car. I use this rule to explain how you
need to deal with *motos*. Chances are you are going to
hit one every now and then. I've personally hit three – or
rather, in my opinion, three have hit me. Each time, the
moto driver was attempting to pass me on the right as I
was stopped or trying to make a right turn. There are no
rules for the *motos*.

This rule applies to road rage, too. Don't ever
let yourself get so angry that you run someone over. I
promise the time will come when you want to run some
moto driver over. Do not do it. If you kill someone, the
government puts you in jail. It is mandatory. Don't kill
someone in an accident. If things get that bad, it is time
for you to go on vacation…

Rule #3 – If you see an AMET, act as if you are
obeying normal traffic laws. The fact is, the AMET do
not really care about the traffic laws. If there is a sign
that says "No Left Turn," see Rule One for when you can
disobey the rule. As long as you do not get hit, you are
fine. Truth is, if there is an AMET there, you can still
turn as long as you "get their permission." Permission
is easy to obtain. All you need to do is turn on your turn
signal and point, making sure your facial expression
signifies that you need to go that way (raised eyebrows
and an eager look). This works best with female drivers,
especially when the AMET is male. The AMET will
often stop traffic to help you turn where you shouldn't be
turning. So the general rule is: the AMET will only give

you a ticket if your registration has expired, or if you are talking on your cell phone while driving. As long as you are not in violation of Rule Five, you should be fine, if you also stay off the phone and wear your seat belt.

Rule #4 – Plan to take an extra thirty minutes to get wherever you're going, because traffic is unpredictable. Dominicans call traffic jams "*tapones.*" No one really knows why a *tapone* happens, but they do. *Tapones* can occur anywhere and at any time. They can be caused by a truck stopping in the middle of the road to unload its cargo. The street may be closed ahead, for some unknown reason, and no one in front of you has figured that out yet. There may be too many people going the wrong way on a one-way street. There may be an accident, a car fire, a bus that is broken down, or a *moto* driver who got hit and is lying in the middle of the road bleeding. The National Police may be doing random searches for guns.

You actually have no clue why the traffic has stopped – it just has. Although you may never know the reason, each of my examples is one I have personally seen. I think the general cause is the AMET and their lack of training on how to control traffic problems. They seem to feel they need to direct traffic physically and personally. They sometimes will stop cars to lecture or talk with the drivers. You never know when there'll be a *tapone*; so just learn to deal with them by always having plenty of time to make your destination.

Rule #5 – If you look like a *gringo*, you are probably going to get some tickets. I have received two tickets for running red lights, which is not a crime unless you are a *gringo*. I have also been ticketed for driving without registration; once again, I think the motivation was my lack of nativeness. The first ticket I got for going through a red light really bothered me. Five cars ran the red light, and I was second in line – three ahead of the last car that went through the light – but I got the ticket. The other one I got was not a concern, because I was able to pay the fine on the spot. I just paid the policeman in cash. I didn't have to sign anything, and I never received anything in the mail. It was a little more expensive than going to the ticket place clear across town, but I was happy not to have to make the trip.

Ana explained that it was not really important if you got some tickets: you could either pay them (they are cheap) or not pay them (the DR has no way to enforce them). I paid the first ticket about six months after I got it. It cost something like RD$60 (US$1.75). Ana had received a ticket a year or so earlier for talking on her cell phone while driving, and it cost about US$15. My ticket for driving without proper registration was issued about two years ago. I haven't been bothered enough to go pay it, so I don't yet know how much it will cost. I have since received my residency, which requires a certificate of good conduct; so I don't believe they have a way to track the ticket. I think I'll leave it unpaid for now.

To me, the driving madness is one of the most aggravating things about the DR. I can deal with the electricity problems because it is hard to assign blame to anyone in particular; but some idiot almost always causes the traffic problems. It's often a selfish driver stopping in traffic to cut into a turn lane. Problems are also caused by a self-centered driver stopping to unload or load cargo or passengers in the middle of the street. My best advice for dealing with the traffic is to suggest you start doing what many Dominicans do, and take a beer with you when you go places. If you get bothered, just pop the top and relax.

If you forget the beer, you could just pull over to , through liquor store and grab a cold one.

You are in a beautiful country. Life here s be laid-back. Getting upset or angry about the half-wit drivers won't do anything but cause you to have a bad day. About the beer: Dominicans don't think there's anything wrong with drinking and driving, as long as you just follow Rules #1 through #5, above. From what I understand, the AMET won't bother you unless you get selfish and won't share. Enjoy!

Becoming Dominican

The longer you live in the Dominican Republic, the more you will realize the importance of plantains and bananas. Dominicans eat bananas in one form or another at every meal. They eat them smashed, fried, fried and smashed, boiled, baked, smashed and baked, and even raw. Dominicans love to see foreigners eating their favorite food and expect them to love it. They will begin to tell you that if you eat enough bananas you will eventually become a Dominican. They will call you *aplatanado*, which means you are turning into a plantain. As you become more accustomed to Dominican culture, you will start to use Dominican slang, you will start to eat Dominican-style food, and you will slowly blend into Dominican society. This section will talk about some of the necessary steps in becoming a real part of Dominican society.

Residency

Every time you leave and enter the country, you have to pay a US$10 tourist visa fee. When you are traveling every other week, this starts to add up quickly. If you plan to enter the DR and not leave for a while, you'll be charged a tax for overstaying your tourist card's duration. This tax is nothing to worry about because it is relatively small. I had to pay RD$500 (US$20) once when I was here for too long; but I am not really sure if that was a real legal fine, or if the agent knew I was just stupid enough to give him the money.

If you plan on working in the DR, you will eventually find it beneficial to obtain a residency card and a Dominican ID, which is called a *cedula*. The residency card allows you to enter the country without paying the tourist card fee. It also allows you to work and stay in the country for as long as you like.

The process for obtaining residency is fairly straightforward, if you read it as a list. However, actually obtaining your residency is a process full of pitfalls if you attempt to do it on your own. You have to go to the Department of Immigration and deal with Dominican bureaucracy. The lines are horrendous. The workers are rude. From start to finish it will take you at least six months, and more than several full days of running from one place to another. If you plan to do it on your own, my recommendation would be to pay the VIP fee whenever possible. This extra fee allows you to skip the longer lines. It also allows you to pick up your card the same day you are approved. Filing for your papers on your own will end up costing you around US$300. Take into consideration that you will have to spend several full days figuring it all out. You'll often have to go and get another document, or change something and come back to fix the error. I do not recommend going it on your own.

I strongly recommend that you have a lawyer help

you with the filing of your residency papers. It will cost about US$1,000, but the time you save is well worth the fee. Using the services of an attorney, you'll be able to take care of the entire process in two visits. During the first visit you will take the blood test and get a chest x-ray. The second visit is to have your picture taken and pick up your *cedula* and residency cards.

Getting Sick for a Month Straight

When I first began coming to Santo Domingo, I was very strict with my water and food consumption. I would only drink water if I saw the bottle opened in front of me. I didn't take ice in my drinks because I feared there were parasites in the ice cubes. I brushed my teeth with bottled water. When I showered, I kept my lips tightly closed, because I had heard horror stories of people getting bugs from the water in the shower. At first my girlfriend protected me, really trying to make sure I had no chance of a parasite entering my body. She reminded me not to drink certain things, and always ordered a special bottle of water unopened for me when we went out.

With regard to food, I was very careful not to eat things that could be contaminated. I only ate fruits whose peel had been removed just prior to my eating them. I would not eat meat or other foods that were not delivered to me sizzling hot. I sometimes skipped meals completely, or skipped parts of meals that did not look or smell exactly the way I thought they should. To me, it was a serious issue. I had seen National Geographic and the Discovery channel with shows on malnutrition, worms, food poisoning, and other digestive problems caused by having parasites or eating contaminated food.

I was probably a little more than cautious: I was on the verge of nervous, and a little scared of becoming infected or sick.

After four or five months of traveling to the Dominican Republic, I began to realize my eating habits were not normal, at least by a typical Dominican's standards. At about the same time, I decided to make Santo Domingo my permanent travel base for work. Right about then, Ana started giving a hard time about how delicate I was. She teased me about being weak and fragile, because my stomach was weak. She giggled when I refused to drink water from an opened bottle, or from a bottle or cup other people had used. Finally, she told me I would always be different if I kept acting differently. She pointed out that she was fine, even though she used tap water for brushing her teeth. She had ice in her drinks and showered without the fear of water entering her mouth. She said that Dominicans seldom had problems from the food or water because they had stronger stomachs. She told me I just needed to start "living Dominican", and if I got sick I would get over it. Once I had been sick, it would never come back. Soon my stomach would be trained to be strong, just as every native-born Dominican's stomach learned to be strong.

My transition to having a strong stomach began with adding ice to my drinks. I learned that the ice is all very similar to ice we buy in bags in the USA. I learned that Dominicans ONLY drink bottled water. In fact, they buy it in five gallon bottles, which is much cheaper than buying it in the twenty-ounce bottles I had been buying. I began to drink water from cups, knowing it really was from a bottle in the kitchen. I started to brush my teeth with the tap water. I even rinsed my mouth out every now and then in the shower.

The first week of the experiment, my life was nothing out of the ordinary. I didn't get sick. In fact, I felt a little silly for having been so strict with myself for so long. My girlfriend laughed at me. As I left to work at the end of the week, I felt fine, and was proud I was becoming Dominican. I could now relax a little, because my stomach was just as strong as the Dominicans' stomachs! I left for the States on Sunday – happy, fit, and proud of my newfound freedom!

Now, I am not a scientist, so I am not sure if it takes parasites a couple of days to grow inside you before they take effect. However, on Monday afternoon, just as I was finishing my lunch I felt a sharp pain in my gut. It felt as if a ten-inch hunting knife had been pushed through my abdomen. It bent me over and almost caused me to cry. I can't explain the sensation other than to say the hunting knife had entered my stomach from the lower right-hand side and every couple of minutes it would twist around, just to remind me how terrible it felt. At first I thought it was something I had just eaten. I headed to the restroom, hoping I could throw up and get it over with. As luck would have it, the pain was actually lower than my stomach; and no matter how hard I tried, I could not make myself throw up. As a result, I had to relieve myself the other way. I ended up spending the rest of the day running back and forth between work and the restrooms.

In Mexico they call it Montezuma's Revenge. In Idaho we call it the Trots. In some states it is called the Hershey Squirts. In my opinion, it does not really matter what you call it. I had it, and bad. Now, keep in mind I am not much for going to doctors; so I spent the entire week at work drinking Pepto-Bismol®. You know I am strong enough to deal with these kinds of things; some little tiny thing had gotten inside my stomach, but that wasn't going to cause me to miss a day of work. As the week went on, I became more and more tender downstairs. Toilet paper began to feel like sand paper. At times I noticed I was bleeding. I am sure I cried several times. I had to put some ointment in the nether regions to make things bearable. During the week, I went through about four bottles of Pepto, and ended up so dehydrated my lips cracked and bled as well. I was messed up.

When finally I got home the following Sunday, things had not progressed at all. I had found if I ate nothing, there was nothing to come out the other end, but this was not a good solution. Whatever was inside me just seemed to want to eat the side of my stomach walls. It was as if it had to eat something, and if I didn't ingest food for it, it was literally going to eat me alive. I had cold sweats. I had hot flashes. My backside was so tender I could hardly sit. I was completely miserable.

In the Dominican Republic, if you get sick to your stomach they will feed you all kinds of concoctions. The first one you'll get will always be a mixture of lime juice and salt. It is very strong, and the first time you take it will make you gag. I drank it, and it made me cry because it burned my stomach so badly. It felt like drinking bleach. I had to head to the restroom almost immediately. If the lime-juice preparation doesn't work they will mix up some other compounds with just about every ingredient you can imagine. I have had raw eggs with onions, some sort of herbal tea, a sweet one that tastes like lemon and honey, and one mixture I did not care to find out about. When you are really sick to your stomach your mind seems to empty out too, and there's a feeling of desperation. You figure it just can't get any worse – and then it does.

Well, I learned something about the lining of Dominican stomachs during my days of uncontrolled bowels. Dominicans' stomachs really are stronger, because they have lived with the parasites their whole lives. *Gringos* need to go to the doctor when they have loose bowels. They should go fast. I ended up being cured by two little pills. I don't know what they were, but they must have killed whatever monster was living in my stomach. It went away, and as it died, it only flared up a couple of times during the next two or three weeks. I am pretty sure my Dominican family believes it was their concoctions that finally did the trick. I am sure my wife thinks my stomach finally got stronger. What I am not sure of is whether it was a good idea or not to go through the pain and suffering to get a stronger stomach.

I can now brush my teeth with tap water; at least, I do it at our house in the Capital. When we are in the countryside, I either use bottled water or brush with Listerine. I know it sounds gross, but I think it's better than getting the Trots. I eat most fruits and vegetables, but I am still a little picky about how they are cleaned. I always have ice in my drinks and am not so worried about the temperature of the food. I still seem to get sick about once a year or so; but that's probably normal in any country you live in, particularly when you travel as much as I do. I just take the Dominican remedies the first day, and if they don't work, I head to the pharmacy and get the two magic pills. Works like a charm.

Rats, Roaches, and Rubbish

If I had started writing this book when I was first visiting the Dominican Republic, this probably would have been included in the section of things that almost made me never come back. However, at that time I didn't anticipate the book, and I did come back; so it just goes in this section about lessons. I mentioned earlier that I grew up in Southern California, and that I have lived in Utah, Idaho, Washington State and Washington DC. I mostly lived within city limits, and we usually had regular trash pick up.

When I was in Idaho going to school, the trailer park where I lived was in the country. This place was about three miles outside of town, with nothing but fields surrounding it. The fields were beautiful wheat, lentils, and beans during the spring and summer. In the late summer and fall, they were wonderful-looking dried lines showing where the tractors had cut the produce. In the winter, the fields were the ugliest mud-ridden mounds of slop you could imagine. Each year, just after the fall harvest and when the weather started to turn cold, our poor little trailer park would get infested with just about every living thing from the fields. We had extra cats, we had rodents, we had bugs, and other wild things roaming around.

As I was falling asleep at night, I could often hear the mice eating underneath my trailer. I could hear a scratching here or there and their cute little squeaks. After a few nights, the cute little squeaks would start to bother me, and I would want to get rid of my new neighbors. To me, there was only one way to take care of the problem. I went to the hardware store and bought about $50 worth of rodent killer and filled the underneath of my trailer with it. Problem solved. I remember a time or two in Utah when we had some mice, so we put little traps down and got them. Since the situation in Idaho was more serious, the gentleman at the hardware store was sure the poison would do the trick. I got the same stuff the farmers put around the silos. It worked like a charm.

Other than those few times, I really cannot remember seeing many rodents while living in the United States. Now, I am sure DC has its fair share of rats roaming the streets, because there are some pretty scummy areas; but I don't remember seeing any.

The first rodent I noticed in the Dominican Republic was running down the side of the road in the Colonial District. I was not running; I was sitting in a chair in front of a store hanging out with my girlfriend and her friends, when I thought I saw a cat running towards us. This animal had a tail about a foot long, and its body was at least as thick as the calf muscle on my leg. It was huge – bigger than a Chihuahua. It was just after I realized it was not a small dog that I realized it was running directly at us. I panicked just a little because this thing could probably cause some serious damage. Can you imagine getting attacked by a house cat? Well, this creature would make that look like a butterfly. I started to stand up, figuring I could use the chair to fight it. I was ready to flip the chair over and try to deflect at least some of its fury. Then, without warning, when it was about ten feet away it suddenly turned and ran into a hole in the side of the building.

To my utter horror, the Dominicans did not even see it! They never even realized it was there. They were in terrible danger, and I needed to make sure they knew there were rats here. You know the saying: "If you see one, there must be a hundred." This store needed some of that poison from Idaho. I grabbed Ana's arm to get her attention, and said urgently, "We have to tell the store owner about this rat so he can get some poison! And he also needs to get a big dog... that thing was HUGE!"

In response, she giggled and answered, "That little thing was harmless." I was completely caught off guard. I had been thinking the Dominicans had not seen the rat, when in reality they all saw it – but it was nothing abnormal for them. It was just another day at the market, nothing out of the ordinary.

Over the next few months I realized how many rats there really are living in the Dominican Republic. I have seen them run across busy streets in the middle of the day. I have seen them run across the tops of fences. I have seen them climb buildings, walls, and piles of garbage. I even saw one running tight-rope style across the telephone lines to get across the street. They are everywhere.

Before I get to the lesson I learned about rats, let me tell you a little bit about rubbish, so you can appreciate the environment that creates a perfect home for the rats. The trash collection methods of the Dominican Republic are very different from those I am used to. There are trash-collection companies in the major cities; but once you are outside the cities, most of the locals simply throw the trash in piles outside their houses. Every now and then, they burn the trash piles. If they have a dog, or if there are dogs living around their house, the dogs will eat any old food. If not, the food just rots until it is burned. This gives any rodents plenty of time to eat, have children, and grow.

In the cities, most businesses and buildings have

regular trash pickup a couple of times each week. My neighborhood has trash pickup twice a week. It is great. Regular trash collection, however, is not the general disposal method. Many citizens just dump their trash in the street in front of their houses. These piles are supposed to be picked up by the local trash collectors, but between the time the trash is dumped and its pickup, dogs and the local poor have time to dig through the trash to see if there is anything they want. The street dogs are simply looking for a meal, while the poor people scavenge anything of value. They take anything made of metal. They save plastic bottles. They scrounge for beer bottles. They rip the bags open, dig around, and then throw the trash on the ground. It is an absolute shame.

The open disposal of garbage in the city is a breeding ground for rodents, roaches, and other pests. All sorts of insects crawl around in the trash. Rats scour the piles for food and at times shelter. These piles of festering garbage offer all sorts of disgusting smells and sights. I have seen whole dead dogs, just thrown in the trash. I have seen mounds of rotting meat, with maggots and flies happily basking in the Caribbean sun. It is common to see rotting fruits, vegetables, and all of the normal table scraps. The longer I live in the Dominican Republic, the more accustomed to these gross sights and smells I become. I run right by them and often do not even notice any longer. I realized this one day when my wife went running with me. She was the one who started to gag over the smell of some really ripe rubbish. I guess I have learned not to smell the bad smells, at least not after the first whiff.

Now, let's turn back to my lesson about rats. As soon as Ana and I moved into our apartment on the third floor of a brand-new building, I noticed rats walking around a trash pile in the field next door. One evening I saw several very active and healthy-looking rats, which made me start to pay attention. A few nights later, I saw between fifteen and twenty rats scavenging food. It was one of the sickest things I have ever seen: they were crawling all over the trash without a care in the world. They acted as if they owned the lot and knew they were safe. The rats came out from holes in the cinderblock walls surrounding the lot. They came out from holes in the ground and from burrows under the trash pile. Just seeing those dirty little creatures made me feel as if there were ants crawling all over my skin. I thought it was only a matter of time before the rats realized people were living in the building right next to them. I was afraid they would start to stop by the neighbors' houses for a little snack every now and then.

As soon as I noticed the rats, I started thinking of all the ways I could get rid of them. I thought about buying some sort of gun and shooting them. This strategy was rather exciting, because it reminded me of the hunting trips I have missed so much since I moved here. While I could probably get away with it for a while, I quickly decided it was not really a good idea because we live right in the heart of the city. I also thought about my prior experience with rodents in Idaho. Since that was a safe and non-threatening way to deal with the situation, I determined it was the best approach.

The next day I went to the local hardware store and bought a lot of poison. I bought enough to make little treats for each of the rats I had seen. My plan was to put some chicken or other food in small plastic bags and then mix in the poison. I prepared about twenty small snacks laden with a toxic potion and readied for the evening feeding time. Around sunset, the rats began to scavenge for food. When I saw the first rat, I threw him a little bag of my special mix. It was amazing: before he could get the treat opened entirely, another rat came from out of nowhere and stole the bag. The poor little rat did not even get any food from that first bag. I kept lobbing my convenient treats over to make sure every one of the rats could have some. Over the next hour or so, I threw bag after bag of my poisonous concoction, until I ran out. It was fun – and at the same time, somehow sickening – watching those dirty little devils come from every direction to get their fill of my treat. They would literally fight for a piece of the chicken or some of the mix. No moms looking out for their young here: it was every rat for himself. Some were so full they looked as if they would pop. Others were only able to get a little of the mix, but were still looking for more.

After they had consumed all of my mix the situation turned desperate. The rats seemed to crave the poison. They would eat the mix and then chase, fight, and attack each other. I listened to and watched the tremendous frenzy until about an hour after dark. The scene slowly grew quiet. Now, I do not know how many rats took part in this feeding frenzy, but I would guess there were close to a hundred.

When my wife came home that night, I was happy to tell her about my noble quest to rid the city of its rats. But Ana said I had made a big mistake. She explained that the rats would eat the poison, and then they would go to their lairs to die. If there were rats that had not tried the poison, they would eat the remains of their fallen comrades. They would then be poisoned and die. Other rats would eat the remains of those dead rats, and the cycle would continue. She warned me about birds. She said dogs might have eaten the remains of the rats and been poisoned. I also needed to be careful, because I later heard a rumor that some Haitians eat rats and could potentially be poisoned as well.

I never really thought about the ramifications of my actions. I had put close to fifteen pounds of poison out for the rats. My main concern afterwards was the smell of the hundreds of dead rats. Fortunately for me, I had several weeks of back-to-back travel scheduled. My wife left our windows closed on the side of the house facing where the rats were attacked, to keep the awful smell out of our house. I never heard anything else about the rats. I just know I'll be really careful if I ever want to kill another bunch of rats.

You're probably wondering if my formula actually worked. Well, since that time I have only seen one rat, and it was climbing over the cinderblock wall on the far side of the property, almost as if it was trying to escape. I don't know more than that. I just know I'll try not to let the rats bother me so much. If three million other people can coexist here with the rats, I guess I can manage, too.

Getting Past Basic Spanish

As I have learned Spanish I have really had some great experiences. One of the most interesting has been discovering how many Dominicans speak English, or at least how many think they speak English. I have had countless people say a couple of words to me in English. Gas station attendants often try a few words of English. Every now and then, people in grocery stores ask me questions in English. Taxi drivers usually know several words and are happy to try them out. Almost everyone wants to try one or two words on you. It is great. I think having that attitude when learning Spanish would be a good way to learn more quickly.

I realized I was really learning Spanish when I approached a missionary lady in the grocery store and said "Hi" to her in Spanish – *"Cómo tu 'ta,"* Dominican style. She looked at me as if I had just tried to grab her. She was speechless, started walking backwards away from me, and in addition to being totally shocked, had no clue how to respond. I realized I was speaking Spanish and changed to English. As soon as she heard my English, her attitude changed and she was very friendly. It was an amazing transformation: from freaked out beyond belief to friendly, in just three seconds.

Another time I realized the importance of good Spanish was when I was trying to get a cab from the airport to the city. It is always a bargaining process, and in some instances it is just short of a physical fight, to convince the taxi employees to get you a cab at less than the published rates, – particularly when you are a *gringo*. The published rates are what they try to charge for a trip from the airport to a hotel. These published rates are very expensive, and are made to look as if they were set prices. The airport taxis are a union, and they rule the airport. If you're not wise to their games and even ready to fight with them, you'll pay the published rate, which in my opinion is just short of robbery.

On this particular day, I approached a *taxista* and said I needed a cab to go to the center of the city. He quoted me a price in US dollars. I said, "We're in the Dominican Republic; I will pay in *pesos*." The price he then gave me in *pesos* was the equivalent of the US dollar price.

My response was: "Look, I live here, and I'm not going to pay the prices you get from the tourists. I will pay local price and nothing more." The look he gave me was incredulous. He simply couldn't believe that a *gringo* had just told him he was going to pay local rates.

Now, I have to point out here our entire conversation had taken place in Spanish. He may not have realized it, but his English was probably about a total of twenty basic words and two or three phrases related to getting clients into the cabs. As soon as I said, "I live here, and I haven't paid the ridiculous prices you charge tourists for years; I will pay 800 *pesos* and not one *peso* more," – it clicked for him.

He laughed and said, *"No hay problema."* He put me in a beat-up cab and told the driver that I was to be charged the local price. We were off. As soon as we were in the cab, the driver started complaining (in Spanish) that the price I was paying was so low he would not be able to eat. I laughed. I replied, "I pay this price every week when I go to the airport. It's interesting that the fare to leave the airport is so much higher than the fare to go out to the airport from the city." I also told him I knew that the city taxis, unlike the airport taxis, are not controlled by a union. There are many companies, and they are very competitive.

The guy complained about how the price of gas was higher and how it had just increased. I said, "It's really weird that your car takes gasoline. Every taxi I have been in here runs on propane." "Mine runs on propane, too," he announced.

I laughed at him. *"Hombre,"* I said, "you know

that the price of propane is a third of the price of gas. You can run your car back and forth from the airport to the city all day long, and it will cost you less that one fare!"

As soon as he realized I knew what I was talking about and was not going to give in to him, he stopped complaining. I said I was happy to talk about the weather, the economy, or the elections, but we were done with gas. He decided just to leave things as they were. I have never again paid tourist rates, and have also never had a discussion about gas prices. I'm perceived as a local, because I can talk and act like a local.

Just Loving Life

While making the transition from a fast-paced American to the slower tempo of an island lifestyle, I have often had to remind myself that life goes on, even though things are not happening as quickly as I am used to. Many times I find myself looking at life from the immediately-present perspective, the "right now", which makes me focus on the Dominican Republic's fair share of problems. When all the little irritations add up to one huge frustration and really start to get under my skin, I try to remember to take a step back and recall what I really love about this place. I have to remind myself that most Dominicans are happier than their North American counterparts. Dominicans are used to the driving problems and the electricity shortages. They are used to things just happening when they happen, rather than on some sort of schedule. Women are used to going to the salon and having it take two to three hours to get their hair washed and dried.

Life here is just different. When I feel that the small

irritations have almost reached a critical mass for me, I remind myself just to love life as it is, instead of focusing on what's not happening quickly enough, or what's not available, in the normal Americanized everyday life of first-world countries.

I have a very long list of reasons why I just love life here, but I'm only going to talk about a couple of them. When you make your transition, I recommend you make your own list of reasons to be grateful for, and appreciative of, life in the DR. Doing so will enable you to look at things from a different perspective. You'll be able to remind yourself why you are here and why this island is unique. It will help you refrain from comparing the electricity and water conditions here with those of New York City. Keeping your Dominican Republic life separate from your first-world life will allow your Dominican experience a chance to become part of you, a part you will grow to love and appreciate deeply.

My list of reminders started out short, but has since grown to be several pages long. One of my favorites, and one I have mentioned many times through this book, is the quality of the fruits and vegetables here. The papaya, mangos, pineapples, bananas, passion fruit, and other tropical fruits are to die for. I absolutely love the different fresh juices. I could probably live the rest of my life drinking fresh juice each day and never need anything else. I remind myself every time I eat an avocado how lucky I am to have it, because in the USA there's no chance I would be able to enjoy something like this. avocados in the US are simply a joke. They are the size of the seeds inside Dominican avocados, and they cost twice as much.

Another of my favorites that is simply not

available to the average American is my housekeeper. In the Dominican Republic, almost everyone, no matter his or her social class, has a housekeeper. This includes just about every income level and life style. Lower-income families have someone to come and help cook and clean a couple of times a week. Higher- income families (middle class) usually have a lady who lives with them, and who cooks and cleans for them every day. When middle-class families have children, they also have a nanny, who cares for the children and generally makes the parents' lives easier. Try that in NYC! Good luck!

Ana and I have a housekeeper who comes to our house a couple of days each week. We don't have her stay at our house because we feel that having someone there all the time would invade our privacy. We also think it would be a waste of money to have someone clean our house every single day, when most of the time no one is there. We use our housekeeper to do the laundry, the cleaning, and she cooks us lunch. It works out perfectly: we can eat at our house those days, and then plan to do things away from home the other days. We expect to have her stay full-time when we have children. I just love to order a specific meal and have it cooked just the way I like it. I tell the housekeeper what time I want to eat, and the food is ready! It would be so different if my wife and I had to take turns cooking; or worse, if I told Ana what to cook for me! We tell the lady what we want, and it is happily made for us. When we are done eating, the table is cleaned, the dishes are washed, and then the kitchen is cleaned. When our housekeeper leaves each day our house is perfectly clean. I love it! It makes me feel like a king!

To look at this from a slightly different perspective,

consider my brother-in-law, Tono. Tono is an engineer, and his income is probably equivalent to the income of an engineer in the US. He owns a small company that does repair work for businesses. He is by no means a rich guy who is building huge buildings, or anything like that. Tono's family consists of himself, his wife, Candida, and their three children. Their house has four bedrooms, three bathrooms, a maid's quarters, and is much busier and bigger than the apartment where Ana and I live. Tono and Candida have a housekeeper who stays with them full-time. She goes home Saturday afternoon to spend the weekend with her family, and returns to their house early Monday morning in time to prepare breakfast for them. Her responsibilities are to cook, clean the house, wash the laundry, iron the laundry, and to make sure the house is in order. She does an excellent job.

Tono and Candida also have a nanny who comes each day to help with the cooking, cleaning, and the children. The nanny has worked with their family for fifteen years. The children do not know anything different. They consider her their auntie, and she treats them as if they were her own children. The parents are able to be very involved in their respective careers and still maintain a well-run household. They explain that having a housekeeper, cook, and nanny are just part of everyday life to them. They feel it is not worth their time to cook or clean the floor, because they are higher-income earners, and can make more money putting their superior skills to use in a different kind of job. They want to be able to relax when they are at home; having house help enables them to do exactly that.

Tono recently decided it would be advantageous to have someone drive him. This is a concept totally foreign to me, but the explanation really makes sense. If I were a Dominican businessman, I would have a driver too. As an engineer, Tono spends a good portion of his day driving from one job to another. He drops in on clients to diagnose a problem; if he has the parts with him, he fixes the problem on the spot. If not, he goes to his office to order or pick up parts. Once he has the parts, he returns to the client's business and fixes the problem. This requires Tono to drive, talk on the phone, and manage many different tasks at once. I've already written about the nightmare of driving in Santo Domingo; but I should remind you that one of the only reasons the police will stop you is talking on your cell phone while driving. As a result, my brother-in-law is forced to use an earpiece and pull over often, so he can make notes about what his clients need.

Tono decided to hire an old associate as his driver. Now he can manage his business without worrying about driving and the hazards of the road. He tells the driver where he wants to go, and the driver takes him there. He no longer has to find parking, which is a significant timesaver for him: the driver just drops him at the door and picks him up when he calls. He doesn't have to worry about his truck being hit or things being stolen out of the back of his truck while he is in the client's workplace. He simply has to manage his business. He can also send the driver for parts, or to pick up other workers.

Having a driver has enabled Tono to be more productive, and to increase the number of jobs he does each month. Now, there are many reasons people in the US do not have drivers, the most important being liability and pay. In the DR, you can easily have your driver covered on your insurance, particularly when you are running an operation with more than one vehicle. It's also very inexpensive to have someone at your beck and call. I believe my brother-in-law pays between $300 and $400 a month to have a driver. I love the DR!

I know of many other people who also use drivers from time to time. They are not the type of people you would expect to have drivers, or who would have drivers in the US. Many moms use drivers so they are able to sit with their children pay attention to them while they are going from one place to another. Many white-collar workers use drivers to save time at the store, running errands, and picking up children from school. This custom is unlikely to become common in the US because of the liability issues and the extreme costs of labor.

Whenever I feel disheartened about the DR and think life would be so much better back in the USA, I think of these luxuries:

- There's no way I could have someone come to my house and cook and clean for me.

- I would never want to have an American nanny; I wouldn't want some inexperienced kid watching my children. In the DR, I'll hire a lady who has raised children before, and who will do what I say.

- In the USA there would be no way I could eat the incredible fruits and vegetables I get here every day.

I remind myself that sacrifices have to be made no matter where you live – but living in Paradise is something to love. If you can learn to overlook the small annoyances and enjoy every minute of the good experiences, you'll get much more out of your life in the Dominican Republic.

Time Is Not an Issue

Most Americans, Canadians, and Europeans have a sense of time. They feel an obligation to be at appointments when they are scheduled. In the US, if you are late somewhere you should plan on having missed your appointment. Try being late to an appointment with your doctor in the US: you will likely be charged for the missed appointment and have to schedule another one. This is probably one of my biggest challenges. If I were invited to a friend's house in the US and told we would meet at 8:00 PM, I would be there at 8:00. If I didn't make it till 8:15, I would probably apologize for being late. If I had a 10:00 AM appointment with a doctor, I would go to the office at 9:30. Arriving at 9:45, I would feel late, because I wouldn't have time to fill out the paperwork beforehand.

In the DR, things are very different. I have been invited to parties that start, or at least are scheduled to start, at 8:00; but when we got there at 10:00 PM, we were the first guests to arrive. When this happened, I felt as if we were imposing, because the hosts were not ready. Once I went to a birthday party with my wife. I had pushed her to "try to be on time for once." She reluctantly agreed to go with me close to the scheduled start time. When we arrived, the hosts were not even home. They were out, and the house help didn't expect them home for at least an hour! I remember a dinner party at my own house; we told people we were going to start at 7:00. People started to show up at around 9:00; we had drinks and snacks and socialized for a couple of hours. The food was not even thought about until close to 11:30 PM, and it was only served then because I was starving. Our guests did not seem to mind the wait. My wife acted as if we were serving people *waaaaay* too early. She told me we should probably wait until 12:30 or so, because our guests were enjoying talking together. I was ready to die of starvation: I didn't realize at that time that Dominicans expect to eat right before they go home. In the US, when I had guests to dinner, we would eat first and then socialize. When we had barbecues, I would have the food prepared, and would put the meat on the grill as soon as my guests arrived. We would then eat, drink, and socialize until they left. The rules of the Dominican Republic seem backward to me.

As a general rule in the Dominican Republic, you shouldn't show up at a party until *at least* an hour after the scheduled start time. If you want to get there along with everyone else, you should make it two hours after the start time. If you want to arrive just in time for the food, you should count on about three hours after the scheduled start. If you get there "on time", expect to find the hosts unprepared. And there's a good chance you'll find no one home except the house-help.

The "correct" time of arrival is very specific, depending on the group and the occasion. For a daytime business meeting you should be punctual, but expect to wait a little. For a casual occasion at someone's home, you should plan on everything happening later than you might expect. For a dressy night out on the town, shift everything to an hour later. Never expect to have things happen when scheduled.

Birthday parties are completely unlike any other event. Most birthday parties are held in a bar or restaurant. People show up whenever they want to. There is no one appropriate time to be there. If you want to go early and hang out, that's fine; or if you want to come later and just dance, that's fine too. This rule applies to the "birthday person" as well. I have been to birthday parties where the guest of honor showed up first, and parties where they arrived way after the rest of the group. I've even been to parties where the birthday person arrived, and then left while all the guests were still partying. The only real rule for birthdays is that the guests are free to go as soon as they have cake. My wife says that if you are hosting a birthday party, you should buy a really excellent cake. And don't serve it until you're ready for the guests to leave; because as soon as you serve the cake, people will go. Many people will also take a slice of cake home for their children, family, or friends – so buy a bigger cake than you think you'll need.

My last time-related recommendation has to do with the lunch hour, or lunch hours. In the USA, it is not uncommon for people to have only a thirty-minute lunch break, particularly if they are working in an office. For a "long lunch," it's fairly common to be able to take an hour. In the DR, the lunch break lasts approximately two hours. Some lunches last anywhere from one to three hours. I still haven't really adapted to this phenomenon. From a lifestyle perspective, I like the concept: Ana and I have time to run errands, relax, and every now and then take a nap during her lunch break.

Working in the DR means adjusting to the expectations of your office. The big difference I have noticed is that Dominicans socialize much more than Americans. They almost never eat alone, and often go home to eat with their family. If it is not possible to eat with family, they will eat with co-workers, friends, or business associates. The one custom is that Dominicans do not eat alone. They take their time with the meal, and talk about life. My in-laws in La Vega get together almost daily for lunch – not just the ones who live together, but also everyone who is able to make it. If this happened in the US, I would think of it as a reunion. In La Vega, it is just lunch with the family. Everyone knows lunch is served at around 1:00, and if they want food they need to be punctual. If they are late (as I explained above), they probably won't get any food. I have seen as many as twenty-five people just "drop in" for lunch. It is something you just have to get used to.

Have an Escape Plan

When I first came to the DR I was fairly new to my job. I had been out of school for just over a year, and I was not really that settled in life. I owned a house in Utah, and I had a vehicle as well. Either my upbringing or my schooling has caused me to be a bit overcautious. As I planned my first visit to the Dominican Republic, I read as much as I could find about it. I spent a couple of evenings researching and reading on the Internet. I also bought several travel books about the Dominican Republic and read their recommendations. My first trip was great, and it went just as planned, with no major issues or problems.

As I mentioned earlier, when I began to make the change from visiting a lot to actually living in the

Dominican Republic, I started leaving a few things there every week. The bag I left with clothes and running gear turned into a suitcase after a month or two. Over the next couple of years, that became two suitcases and a gym bag. I had read a good deal on the Internet about how every Dominican wanted to get out of their country and would do just about anything to live in the United States. I entered the relationship with Ana very cautiously because of all those stories on the Internet.

I also planned to test her frequently, to make sure there was nothing weird or underhanded going on. One of my tests was to leave things in my suitcase to see if it was ever gone through. I would leave some money, maybe some candy or gum, and almost always a watch. I had read early on that these were the kinds of things that would go missing quickly. The money could easily simply disappear. The candy or gum would be eaten, and would never be worried about. I don't know what the reason for leaving the watch was. My bag was never gone through.

When we started to get more serious, I tested Ana by giving her some money to "hold" for me while I was away. I had her open a bank account just for my money, and every now and then I made a deposit of a hundred dollars. My excuse was that I was saving money, so I could have money to spend when I was there. Really, I wanted to see if money was ever taken out of the account when I was not there. After several months during which the money just built up, I gave her a Visa card and an American Express card, each with an initial limit of about two thousand dollars. That wasn't much, in my opinion, to allow me to test her thoroughly and find out what she would do with my money or my credit. My theory was

that if she sneaked a pair of shoes or a shirt on the cards
here or there, then I needed to be careful. If she ever put
a large amount of money on them, I would cancel the
cards, and call it a good lesson as I initiated the escape
plan described below.

What actually happened? Ana never even activated
the cards until we had been dating for almost a year. I
had to do it for her, and then tell her she had to use the
card to pay for something for me. She has since said she
really appreciated that I gave her the cards, because she
knew it was a sign I trusted her. She said she would never
use them. She was often more worried about losing one
of my non-activated cards than she was about her entire
purse.

My initial escape plan was never to leave anything
in the Dominican Republic that I couldn't just walk away
from if something bad happened. I figured about two
hundred dollars' worth of clothes and a bag were enough
to show I was coming back; but also not so much that it
would bother me just to throw them away if we had an
issue. Luckily, I never had to go through that ordeal.

Besides keeping a minimum amount of assets in
the Dominican Republic, I also protected my assets in the
United States. I rented my house out and hired a property
management company to take care of it. I lent my car to
my sister and only used it when I was there. My excuse
for her was that I needed her to drive it to keep it running
smoothly. In reality, I knew she needed a car; it was a
win-win situation. It was perfect for both of us: she got
an extended test drive on the car, and I had the comfort of
knowing I had a vehicle to fall back on, if my plans in the
Dominican Republic didn't work out.

After about a year and a half, my sister bought my

car. She called me to tell me she felt she should be paying me rent on the car. I told her I was thinking about selling it so I could have a down payment for a house in the DR. We figured out how much it was worth and worked out the sale. I sold the car without having to deal with buyers or dealers. She bought a car she had practically owned for almost two years, and loved it.

What are my recommendations to anyone who asks about moving here? First, and most importantly, you need to be sure you can live here and like it. I strongly recommend that you come down for a six-month trial run before you make any long-term arrangements. You also need to think about the different scenarios and how you will deal with them. Never put all your eggs in one basket and move to a foreign country without an escape plan. Always have somewhere to go and enough money to get back on your feet, as a minimum. I actually had much more than that when I came here. I was making great money. I had a house, a car, and plenty of credit to use to get restarted if I ever needed to leave. I also put money into investment real estate and saved money in investment accounts, because I was actually spending less living here than I would have been had I lived like most of my colleagues. I was living a great lifestyle, but on a limited budget, and I had the savings and security of knowing I could get out if it was ever necessary.

PART TWO

Part Two is different from Part One because it contains more about general strategies for making the move to the Dominican Republic, and less of my personal story. I'll provide you with several guidelines to help you move forward.

Part Two is all about you and how you can do this. I'll give specific tips I think will benefit you. I will talk about how to overcome difficulties, and how to make this transition as easy as possible. I assume you are an adult; so I will explain things as directly and clearly as I can. You can take my advice as gold and follow it, or you can decide I am totally nuts and do something entirely differently. I'll never know, so do as you please.

Choosing Your Airline

One of the inevitable facts about moving or traveling to the Dominican Republic on a consistent basis is that you are visiting an island. You're going to need to decide on the optimal way to reach the DR from your home, or wherever you plan to visit. Many Dominicans have family in the United States, and it is not uncommon for Dominicans to make an annual trip to visit their family. It is very common for Dominicans living in the US to spend a month each year back in the Dominican Republic with their friends and family. I have several new uncles who seem to be in the DR more than they are in New Jersey, where they work, have houses, and families. I travel at least four times a year to visit my own family, and have spent at least thirty weeks traveling for work each year.

Since the DR is an island, you need to get used to flying several times a year. I am an Internet junkie who has spent several hundred, if not thousands, of hours researching airline tickets. As a general rule, I believe flights from the East Coast cost in the neighborhood of $300-$500 round trip. West Coast trips tend to run about $700. When you go to Canada, the cost jumps significantly; and from anywhere other than North America, it really starts to climb.

I recommend you research the airline that serves the area you plan to fly to most frequently, and stick with that one airline. I make this recommendation because typically prices are better on airlines that have a lot of flights in and out of a certain airport. Also, by being loyal to one airline, you will become one of their Preferred Customers; and as a Frequent Flyer, you'll begin to get additional perks, upgrades, and special check-in lines. Although these are little things, they do add up when you travel a lot. Once you have Elite Access as a Preferred Customer, it is worth paying $150-$200 more to fly with your preferred airline. This is because Elite flyers get to carry more bags, they earn additional points for free flights, and oftentimes they'll be flying First Class. During the past four years, I have had the mileage to become a Platinum Frequent Flyer on both Delta and American. I have also flown all the other airlines, and have some opinions about which airline is the best choice.

Here is a side point I really need to emphasize: once you begin to live on an island, you will learn what you miss from home. Every time you travel, you'll find yourself bringing more and more back with you. As you gain Dominican friends and families, they'll begin to give you shopping lists of the things they miss or want from the outside. For example, I have a standing mandate to bring chocolates back. Nothing special: just a trip to Wal*Mart, and one of those bags of small chocolate bars for each of my wife's siblings. Four bags of chocolates mandatory every trip means about fifteen pounds of chocolate in my suitcase. It also means fifteen fewer pounds of room. If I didn't have Elite Access, I would have a fifty-pound limit. Depending on the airline, I would also have a limit of zero to one free bag. I am Elite on both Delta and American, so I can carry up to three checked bags that weigh up to seventy-five pounds each. I need to point out that it has never been my intention to max this limit out; nevertheless, it has happened on many more occasions than I would like to admit.

On any flight to the Dominican Republic, it's easy to tell who is the Dominican and who is the tourist. All you need to do is look at who has more overloaded duffel bags coming off the carousel at the baggage claim. Look for who has more grocery bags, backpacks, diaper bags, carry-on suitcases, and a box for carry-on as they board. That is a true Dominican. They will complain that the overhead bins are not big enough, as they shove in their hundred pounds of carry-on goodies. (The extra cost to fly with an airline with which you have preferred status is worth it, because you will likely fly first class, and not have to hear the locals complain about how little space they have to store their carry-ons.)

I think you should consider two things: price and schedule. It's not worth saving $150 on your airline fare if you have to spend an extra night midway in your travels. It's not worth saving $100 if you have to pay $50 per checked bag and you travel with two checked bags. Pay attention to all the extra charges, and you'll soon find out that being a Preferred Customer really does have its rewards.

Here are my opinions about each airline:

Delta Airlines

In late 2008, Delta and Northwest Airlines merged, so what I say about Delta here will include Northwest. In my opinion, of all the airlines, Delta treats their Elite customers best. They have the best upgrade and rewards program, and they actually do give those who fly regularly better treatment than once-a-year flyers. If I have a choice of Delta and any other airline for the same price, I always fly Delta. Because I am a Platinum Frequent Flyer with free upgrades, I have only flown coach on a Delta flight about three times during the past two years, even though I have taken close to three hundred Delta flights.

Delta has been best in making connections, getting their flights out on time, and having my luggage actually show up with me. The only exception is when I am flying on Delta for the first part of a connecting flight, then switching to another airline before my final destination. If that's the case, forget it. Your bag will show up sometime next week. Put as much of your stuff as possible into your carry-on; you'll be on your way home before your checked bag arrives.

In Santo Domingo, Delta experiences very long lines for economy travelers. If you are flying Delta, I recommend you arrive about two and a half hours early so you can beat the rush. If you're flying to Atlanta, get there three hours early; you'll have to wait in line behind the JFK passengers who are leaving about forty minutes before you. If you are a Frequent Flyer or are flying First Class, you can probably cut thirty to forty minutes off your arrival time at the airport. I have made it through cutting it as close as an hour, but I don't recommend that. One of my biggest travel comforts is making sure always to have plenty of time.

When I first started going to the Dominican Republic, it seemed that I was the only Frequent Flyer on many flights. I would be all alone in First Class, or with just one or two other passengers. They used to have fairly good food with a choice steak or ribs for the meat, or some sort of pasta with chicken. First Class on Dominican Republic flights is not like International First Class or International Business Class, because the planes are not the really big ones. The flights are only three to four hours, and you don't really need to lie all the way down to sleep, because you're not going to get a full night's sleep in any case.

Like everyone else in recent months, the airlines have been making cutbacks in an effort to get their budgets under control. One of the first things to go was in-flight meals, in most cases even for First Class patrons. Delta now serves a paper-wrapped sandwich to its First Class customers. American Airlines has chosen to offer various items for sale from a "bistro cart"; and personally, I would prefer it if Delta did something similar. Well, at least I'm not sitting in the back being handed a terrible microwave meal. I'll just skip the sandwich, ask for a cold drink and some chips, and relax.

During the past year, Delta has completely revised its fee structure. They now charge for flight changes and use of reward points for tickets, along with various other new add-on fees. In my opinion, this is one of the major disadvantages of Delta. I recently missed a flight on Delta; we had used reward points for my wife's ticket to fly with me. We had to pay the exact amount we originally paid for the ticket to be able to use the ticket the next day. On another recent flight, I had booked to fly from Las Vegas to Salt Lake City on a Friday. The conference I was attending canceled the Thursday events, so I could leave a day early. The fee for me to change the flight was $385. If I missed that flight, it would cancel the entire rest of my trip, and I would lose the $800 I had already paid in fares. In the end, I was able to change the ticket for another less heavily-booked flight, and to fly for only $185, but I was not happy. "Ridiculous" is an understatement for how I feel about Delta's new fees. If American or one of the other airlines gave the same upgrade preferences, I wouldn't fly Delta again.

American Airlines

When you begin traveling to the Dominican Republic – or anywhere in the Caribbean, or Central or South America – you will quickly learn that American Airlines has a monopoly on the market. They have by far the best travel schedule, with flights out of Santo Domingo about nine times daily. You can fly direct to Miami, New York, Boston, or Puerto Rico. If you need complete flexibility, then American Airlines is the way to go. You'll almost always be able to find a flight out.

The downside of traveling only on American Airlines is they are a truly global airline. It is not uncommon for their top-tier Frequent Flyers to have several hundred thousand miles of travel every year. As a result, flying fifty or sixty flights with them each year is not enough to warrant special treatment. I feel that they treat their customers less professionally than Delta. With American, I haven't really had the same positive experiences that Delta has given me with upgrading friends and family or other bonuses. On top of that, American Airlines' fleet is much older in general than the fleets of most other airlines. I read somewhere that their planes were built (on average) sometime during the 1980s. I don't know if that is really true; but, based on their choice of colors for seat covers, carpets, and décor, I'd say they might have been built in the 1970s.

American Airlines knows they control the market in the Dominican Republic, so their flights are not consistently priced. Sometimes they have great deals, and other times they'll be more expensive by far than other carriers. If you are going to use American Airlines exclusively, make sure you always check the other flights to see if you are being gouged. They do have excellent flight availability out of Miami and Puerto Rico, so they're great when you need to go to the West Coast.

My final complaint about American Airlines concerns their seeming inability to get flights out on time. This does not seem to be a real problem for the flights leaving the Dominican Republic; but almost every time I have flown out of Miami, I've had to sit on the plane for an hour waiting for takeoff. For example: Flight 1911 from Miami to Santo Domingo on Sunday evening is scheduled at something like 7:30 PM every week. This flight is scheduled to land in Santo Domingo at around 9:30 PM. However, I've taken this flight about twenty times, and have yet to arrive in Santo Domingo before 10:30. I know a frequent traveler who takes that flight fifty-two times each year (yes, that's every week). He once told me that in the five years he has taken that flight, he only remembered taking off on time a handful of times. Now, he plans to show up to the airport late. He figures if it *is* ever on time and he misses it, he'll just get the first flight out Monday morning.

Aside from all my negative comments about American Airlines, they do offer upgrades to their Frequent Flyers. It is just harder to use them, and you are not automatically upgraded. You can earn miles towards reward tickets. American's reward tickets are better than Delta's: they start at five thousand fewer miles for the low-reward tickets, and they have lower fees, especially if you need to change a ticket from one day to another. American is also the only airline that flies to the United States that has a Club or lounge in the airport in Santo Domingo. The lounge is nothing special, but it offers free drinks and some snacks. The best thing about it is that it's much quieter than waiting by the gate.

The Other Airlines

The other main airlines that fly from the US to the DR are not airlines I take frequently enough to be able to give them big recommendations. Continental is the airline I have been most impressed with overall. They have great First Class service in comparison to the other airlines, and they have incredible First Class lounges in their main airports. I find that Continental's flights usually cost more than the other airlines, so I rarely fly Continental.

United is the worst of all the airlines. Its planes are old. Their staff is more than rude, and they have very poor connections out of the Dominican Republic. Skip United when possible.

Jet Blue is another airline I recommend people skip. They are the international version of Southwest, except that they don't emphasize saving money on fares, as their parent company does. Jet Blue offers several flights from the East Coast to the Dominican Republic daily. However, they charge fees for checked luggage, and they have some of the most restrictive luggage rules of any airline. Once I connected through Newark to take a flight on Jet Blue to Santo Domingo. I had flown in on Delta; since the airlines are not friends, I had to go and pick up my luggage at Delta's baggage claim and then get on a tram to go to Jet Blue's check-in counter. When I got there, the ticket agent told me I couldn't check the mirror I had purchased during the week – a simple bathroom mirror in a box. Both the size and the weight met posted guidelines for checked items. The ticket agent informed me that Jet Blue did not allow people to check boxes to the Caribbean. Since my mirror was new, still in the box, it was prohibited. She wanted me to leave the mirror with her and said she would dispose of it for me. Before I would give her that brand-new mirror, I would jump up and down on it a hundred times! In the end, I persuaded a manager to let me pay an exorbitant fee to check the box. I had to sign a waiver of responsibility in case the mirror broke – but it arrived safely.

I have since tried never to fly Jet Blue. I've also done my best to let friends and family know about their severe baggage policy. By the time you pay their extra handling fees for baggage, you'd be better off paying two or three hundred dollars more to fly on a real airline. Besides, you really don't need to collect points that are only good on Jet Blue and Southwest, do you? Not me! I'll take a cold turkey sandwich in First Class over that any day!

Travel Tips

Arrive early. I always arrive exactly two hours ahead of the scheduled departure time, even though I don't have to wait in the long lines for economy class. If I had to fly economy I would probably plan to get to the airport two and a half hours ahead. In the case of a flight before 8:00 AM, two hours in advance would be enough. This applies to both the United States and Dominican Republic flights. I would rather be there early and read for an extra half hour than be late and have to run, or even worse, miss my flight. Arriving with plenty of extra time allows me to relax and catch up on emails or reading. I'd rather relax than stress about the flight any day.

Eat at home before you leave for the airport. I hate the food in the Santo Domingo Airport. I would rather go hungry than eat the awful food they serve there. I have eaten at every food establishment in the airport, and in my opinion, the only edible food is at the stand in Terminal A (get a plain sandwich). The rest of the food should not be served to the public.

I remember one time that I arrived early for my flight, as I usually do; and then the flight was delayed, due to a storm. I wound up sitting in the airport for close to four hours and I was literally starving.

Against my better judgment, I went to the newest food establishment located in Terminal B next to the Duty Free shops and asked about the food they serve.

Now, this restaurant is set up cafeteria-style: you pick up your tray and your drink at the beginning of the counter; and as you go down the counter, you choose things you want to have put on your plate. You get to see the food and make sure it at least looks edible before they give it to you. Well, the first food I saw was desserts. I always skip dessert. The second food I went by was some sort of macaroni salad that looked about a week old. No, thanks, I'd pass on that. When I got to the section of hot food, I had one choice for the starch: white rice. Okay, sold: I would have white rice. I would have preferred rice and beans, or *moro*, or potatoes – but today my choice was plain white rice. Perfect! After deciding I would have plain white rice, I was able to choose my meat from five leftover chicken parts or a huge pile of delicious-looking beef. I thought they had probably just brought out the beef, and I was looking forward to trying it – it looked terrific. There were nice-sized chunks of beef in a rich-looking sauce. I thought I'd ask for a little extra sauce so I could mix it in with the plain rice.

Before I go any further, I need to point out something about ordering food from public establishments. You should always be aware of how new or fresh food is. You should also consider what all of the hundreds of other guests order. If absolutely no one is ordering the excellent-looking beef, there MUST be a problem. If the terrible-looking chicken is consistently chosen, even when they're piling up ten to fifteen tiny pieces including skin and bone, to fill an order, but the beef remains untouched – that's a HUGE RED FLAG! Never assume the huge pile of untouched flesh is new, just because it is bigger than the other piles.

Being a world traveler and partial Dominican, I

decided it was prudent to ask about the meat, so I asked what kind of meat it was. The guy responded: *"Es hígado muy bueno."* I got the *muy bueno* part, but wasn't so sure about the *hígado* part; so I asked, *"¿Qué es hígado?"* He said it was a kind of beef. GREAT! It was exactly what I thought: a fresh pan of succulent beef, ready for me to devour. Not wanting to get something I did not like, I baited the worker. I asked him, "Is it good?" He responded with a huge smile. "Yes, this is my favorite kind of beef!"

Looking back now, I realize I should have turned and walked away. Asking the guy selling you something if it is good is one of the worst ideas ever. But I was very hungry, so I ordered *hígado*, and a lot of it. I could already almost taste the mouth-watering, fresh, juicy, steak-like pieces of beef. Oh, yeah, this was going to be one of my weekly stops at the airport! A huge pile of fresh beef at only US$17.00! How could I go wrong? Top-quality beef was expensive, so this was a bargain.

I sat down at the closest table, put my bag down, grabbed a fork and took a huge bite. Just as my mouth ripped the meat off the fork, my nose noticed something queer about the smell of that gorgeous piece of steak I was about to devour. I chomped down in a serious manner. By the time my teeth had opened and repositioned the meat for the second chew, the juicy flavor and the dry texture of the meat disguised by the dark sauce registered in my brain. This was not steak – it was LIVER! I immediately gagged. My stomach turned and I felt like vomiting. I was the only idiot who didn't know enough Spanish to skip the liver. I'm sure one of the cooks was sitting back in the kitchen laughing at all the *gringos* who ordered that stuff. They had disguised it by cutting it like *fajitas* and covering it with a thick, rich gravy. The onions were sautéed just like you would expect with *fajita* meat, but this was definitely not *fajita* meat.

The helpful server had completely covered my white rice with a thick layer of the sauce, which by now looked to me like diarrhea. I couldn't even eat one bite. It was disgusting. I washed my mouth out with some Diet Coke; ate a couple of tablespoonfuls of Tabasco-drenched rice to try to burn the shit-like flavor out of my mouth, and threw the whole plate of food in the trash. The only thing I could think was, "Why the hell doesn't the Santo Domingo Airport have pizza?" I couldn't wait to get to civilization and be able to order a slice of pizza or a hamburger.

Now I always make a quick sandwich at home and bring it with me. If my flight is delayed, I eat it. If not, I sometimes chuck it. It's better for me to waste a couple of sandwiches every now and then than to risk having a huge plate of organ meats served up to me unknowingly.

<u>Taxis</u>. You are likely going to have to deal with taxis at least twice when you visit the Dominican Republic: once when you arrive, and again when you return to the airport. On arrival in the Santo Domingo airport, I always head upstairs to the check-in desk. I then get one of the taxi drivers up there to work me a deal. It's good for him, because they get less business and are more willing to work with the price. It's also nice for me, because I don't get mobbed as I would in the normal taxi area downstairs.

When you leave the country, have your hotel or a friend call a taxi from the city to take you to the airport. Make sure you ask for one that is comfortable and has air conditioning. You don't necessarily have to use the air conditioning; but if their air conditioning works, you know they do at least some maintenance on their taxi. I have been in taxis that have holes in the floor so large that you could likely touch your foot on the street. I have been in cars with plastic bags taped in the windows. I have ridden in taxis whose doors were completely missing their inside surface. Never underestimate a Dominican taxi company: if the vehicle moves, they will try to charge you to ride in it. If you feel the car is not going to make it all the way to the airport, tell the driver you want a different car. Make them get you one that is adequate – but remember, there is no such thing as a new taxi. It seems as though a car has to be thoroughly tested before it is considered worthy to become a Dominican taxi. The taxi testing process is rigorous. The cars are driven until they are too hammered for normal people to drive, and then they are converted into taxis. This usually means your taxi will have around two hundred thousand miles on it. No, there are no new ones.

When you are in the taxi, be aware of yourself. Don't flash a wad of money; don't openly wear expensive jewelry or watches. I have never personally had a problem, but I also make sure I look just like an average person when I get in the taxi. If I have ten thousand dollars in my pocket, they have no idea, because I wear jeans and a t-shirt. I never wear a watch to the airport. My cell phone is an older model, and I never converse more than chit-chat with the driver.

One last point: make sure you get the unit number of the cab and its color when you order the cab in the city. Other companies like to come in and pirate fares from the more reputable companies. I don't like the pirate cabbies because their cars are not as reliable and they don't work for reputable companies. In my opinion, they are not as safe as a well-reputed company. I always use Anacaona, and have never had a problem or been given a hard time by their drivers.

No flashy jewelry. The longer I live in the Dominican Republic, the more I realize that there really is a different standard for *gringos* and for Dominicans with regard to jewelry. If you're a gringo, I think you are best advised never to wear any jewelry that costs more than $50. This is because as a *gringo*, you already stand out. You also are already a target to some extent. It is not that wearing something expensive is going to guarantee you will have problems, but I believe it increases your odds. When I first came to the Dominican Republic I wore a really nice Rolex watch I had been given as a gift. It was a fake, but no one, even dealers, could tell the difference. I happily wore that watch around for about a year, never thinking twice about it. If someone had wanted it, I would just have given it to them.

The problem was not that the watch would be stolen, but rather that certain people would want to get to know me because they thought I had tons of money. I was targeted by all the street vendors. I was a target when we went to the beach. All kinds of people were asking me for money or to buy something from them. When I quit wearing the flashy watch, I began to blend in more. I know and have observed many wealthy Dominicans, who wear Rolexes, huge diamonds, expensive glasses, rings, bracelets, and all sorts of flash; but this is their country, and the rules are different for Dominicans than they are for a *gringo*. I once asked a Dominican man with a very expensive watch if he ever worried about wearing it. He replied with a smile, "No – if someone tries to take it, my driver will shoot them for even thinking about it. I always have a gun with me." The double standard for *gringos* and Dominicans is created because it is very common and easy for a Dominican to carry a gun. It is more difficult for a *gringo,* and *gringos* are less likely to actually shoot someone over a watch. As a result, I no longer wear a watch at all when in the Dominican Republic.

<u>Platinum American Express</u>. I have spoken about my use of two credit cards. Before I traveled as much as I do now, I would just sign up for any card that would get me miles or points or cash back, but with no annual fee. I now think the Platinum American Express is the card to carry. Even if you only use it for travel, it is worth the $400 fee they charge. With this card, you are able to gain access to almost every airport club. When you fly Delta, you get the Crown Room, and when you fly American you can go into the President's Club. These clubs or lounges are great, because they are usually less busy than the airport. You can sit on a comfortable chair. You can read newspapers and magazines without charge. You can snack on their snacks or get a drink from their bar. It is very comfortable. Internet access is available, and sometimes you can get a free day pass; otherwise, a day pass only costs a few bucks.

If you have a problem with a flight, agents for the airline are available in these lounges and are happy to help you change your flight. They will call the gate for you to find out when the delay will be over. They can have your bags pulled from checked luggage if you decide not to take a flight. These agents are wonderfully helpful, so be very nice to them. On occasion, they have put me in First Class, even when I was not one of their Frequent Flyers. I have had them help me with ticket changes, put me on a new flight when my previous flight was canceled, and I have had them get my luggage when I decided to drive rather than stay in the airport overnight.

One of the downsides to this card is that it's a charge card, not a credit card, so you have to pay the balance every month. Just use what you can afford to pay each month, nothing more. You get miles that accumulate toward free tickets on your choice of airline. They also have other perks; but you'll have to find out from American Express what they are, because they're not paying me for this huge plug, and I don't care to look all the perks up on their web page. My recommendation is, if you don't have a Platinum American Express card, get one.

Safety

When I first came to the Dominican Republic, I almost felt that everything was spinning around me. Things were so different from what I was used to! I was literally on sensory overload, with all the new smells, colors, and especially the sounds. The Dominican Republic is a very noisy country. Besides the different language that surrounds you and seems to be buzzing incessantly inside your head, there are always sirens, car alarms, thumping radios, horns blaring, noisy *motos* racing by, and a plethora of other noises. I had to take one step at a time with regard to safety. I had recently lived in Washington DC, so I was no newcomer to big cities, where you protect yourself with a general lack of trust for those around you. I approached my Dominican experience with the same caution.

In preparation for my travels, I read quite a bit about the Dominican Republic on the Internet and in the news. I found claims of severe violence from crimes, robberies, in-home invasions – and the list could go on continuously. However, I don't believe everything I read on the Internet; so I did a little more research and had a very difficult time finding any verifiable statistics about the actual number of violent crimes versus residents for the Dominican Republic. In fact, many of the articles I read were written by a purported victim of a crime or a friend relaying the story of a victim. Even those articles I found in the newspaper rarely told enough of the story for me to be able to determine if the crimes were simply stories of the individual being in the wrong place at the wrong time, or whether they actually had some sort of culpability in their injury.

Let me explain. In just about every city in the United States, there are areas where I simply would not walk at night. In fact, in every major city in the world you can find pickpockets, muggings, and other smaller, less violent crimes. These crimes often follow a pattern for the individual area, and the victims are picked out because of certain traits or characteristics. Most perpetrators really do not know how much money a victim may have in his wallet or her purse. They just assume that if a person is dressed a certain way, there is enough to make it worth a hold-up. I believe this is the same in the Dominican Republic. Most muggings are done more or less randomly, with certain characteristics making certain victims more favorable than others. I also believe in-home invasions, robberies, and burglaries occur at roughly the same rate as in the United States.

Several differences I see in the Dominican Republic in comparison to most cities in the US is that a large majority of US homes do not have actual crime-prevention doors, steel window coverings, or other deterrents. In fact, most building codes and fire codes require that the front entrance to any building within city limits has to be able to be opened with a minimal pressure of sixty pounds per square inch. That is why in the movies and TV cop shows you see them using the battering ram to open the front door. This code is intended to allow the Fire Department to enter. There are also regulations that would not allow windows to be completely barred up like a prison, because in case of a fire, the people inside would be trapped. It's very different in the Dominican Republic. For one thing, most buildings are built out of cement and rebar (concrete reinforced with steel bars), which are both materials that do not burn; so the fear of dying in a house fire is much lower. Most gas tanks for cooking are kept outside the house, and the valve is usually shut off when the stove is not in use. This is a somewhat primitive means of fire protection, but it is very effective.

A second difference is the amount of security placed on buildings. Most of the homes in the Dominican Republic have actual steel bars over the windows. They also have solid steel doors with several deadbolts, and the house is made of cinderblock filled with rebar and concrete. I believe many houses here are probably better protected than many bank vaults in the US. I know in the case of my house, you could probably ram my front door with a pickup truck, and you would still have a hard time getting in. All this is to say that Dominicans are very protective of their homes. Most in-home robberies are done by an inside job where the maid or housekeeper gives a key to someone outside the household, or the owners trust the wrong person who tells someone how to get in. It is rare to hear of a case where the steel bars are cut or the doors are pried open.

Another difference I see in the crime rates between the DR and the United States – and most of the first world, for that matter – is the entire lack of random killings. I have never heard of a person going into a mall or theater and opening fire on innocent civilians. In the US, there are all sorts of stories in which people use assault weapons to randomly kill as many as they can. It is not uncommon to hear similar stories in Europe. The number of "terrorist"-related random killings is constantly growing. The Dominican Republic, in my opinion, has stayed clear of all that because it is too small for terrorist organizations to want to target.

One of the most noticeable differences between life in the first world and in the Dominican Republic is that here I often see those who have to be ready for war. That is, they carry a pistol when they have a lot of money with them. They keep a gun or two in their car, just in case someone tries to steal the car. Many instances where an individual thinks he can make an easy buck by stealing something are stopped the instant the robber realizes he's going to get some resistance. If you think back to my story from the beach earlier, the whole problem ended as soon as two of my friends pulled out pistols, cocked them, and pointed them in the faces of the supposed police. As soon as they saw there was going to be some serious resistance, and likely at least one of them was going to leave severely wounded, they backed down fast.

My recommendations with regard to safety are very simple. Still, I'll try to focus on several areas of everyday life and how to approach them with caution and safety in mind. The general rule is to try to look like everyone else by dressing similarly and plainly. Remember that there is safety in numbers, and stay out of unsafe areas. To know how to look like everyone else you just need to look around you. When I first came to the DR, I always wore shorts and sandals. Most Dominicans only wear shorts and sandals to the beach or to a pool. If you're going to the beach or a pool, these are appropriate clothes. If not, then you need to dress differently to blend in.

Dominican men wear jeans when they dress casually, and they wear slacks or khakis almost all the rest of the time. Dominican men often wear dress shirts, even if they are dressed casually. It is not uncommon to see men hanging out with their friends in slacks, dress shoes, and a dress shirt, often with a tie. They are dressed better than their North American counterparts. If you are going out for the evening it is appropriate to dress well. You are welcome in slacks or nice jeans and a dress shirt, or even a suit. It will be rare for you to be the best-dressed person at a party, because many Dominican men always wear a suit. I tend to be on the more casual side of dressing up when we go out. I wear dress shoes, jeans, and a dress shirt. I have purchased quite a few Dominican-style dress shirts and wear them often. It is often difficult to tell me from my friends. There's a recent fashion trend among many younger Dominican men of wearing jeans and polo-type shirts. This is acceptable as well, if you fit into that category.

I think women here dress a little "classier" than most North American women. They almost always wear high heels, and they are always dressed up with earrings, makeup, and their hair done perfectly. I rarely see a Dominican woman walking around in casual clothing. Dominican women dress as if they were in a fashion show every day of the week. They have to have shoes that match their handbag and earrings, or they're not fit to leave the house. My wife explains that it is a woman's responsibility always to look beautiful when she leaves her house, even if she is only running to the grocery store. For casual occasions, women in the DR also wear jeans. Women's dress standards seem to be a little more relaxed than the men's standard. I think as long as they feel that they look sexy, they feel they are good to go. I should add that I cannot remember the last time I saw a Dominican women out around town wearing tennis shoes. It just does not happen. They go out in sandals, but not tennis shoes.

My last point about dress is your jewelry. I take the minimalist perspective. As a man, I can get away with nothing except my wedding band, and that is all I wear. Women need to look beautiful, so they need other accessories. My recommendation is not to go with diamonds, pearls, and other high-end and highly expensive items. You can look just as beautiful with an inexpensive jewelry set, and you become much less of a target. All this, of course, depends somewhat on the company you keep and your mode of transportation.

Everyday Life Around Town. When you are out and about during the day it should be life as usual. I don't worry about going most places as long as I am obeying the above rules. I don't carry a lot of cash with me; so if my wallet is taken, I just call and turn off my credit cards and I'm fine. For women, if you are going to carry a purse, you should keep it under your arm. If you are walking next to the street, you should put it on the shoulder away from traffic. I cannot count the number of times I have heard about a *moto* driving past and simply grabbing the purse from a woman, then driving off. It is something that cannot completely be prevented, so just be aware.

Another piece of advice I heard from my Dominican Auntie is: if you are carrying valuables, you should put them in a plastic grocery bag and carry it in the hand opposite to your purse. She told me of a time when she had close to three thousand dollars in cash in a grocery bag, and an empty purse clutched under her arm. The thieves stole the empty purse and left the grocery bag she had dropped sitting right next to her. The more you guard something, the more the thief will want it and ignore the other item.

When you are in public, make it a point never to be the loner. If you're alone, you are an easier target. My sister-in-law, Yolandita, was waiting for a bus after school one day and didn't notice that everyone else had gotten on another bus. As she was sitting there alone, two young men came up behind her and stole her handbag by force. Had she been aware that she was alone, she could easily have walked to another bus stop, or stayed far enough away from the young punks to have been safe. She was busy listening to her IPod and not being aware of her surroundings. (The attackers probably thought the IPod alone was worth stealing her purse, and that was possibly the reason she became a target.) In addition to trying never to be entirely alone, I try not to get in the middle of very large groups, particularly groups demonstrating or protesting. Besides the risk of violence related to the group, I am not comfortable with people touching me from all sides, so I do my best to stay out of these situations.

Just as a point of interest, let me add that Dominicans are much more comfortable with the lack of space than I am. If you are waiting in line, it is very common for the person behind you to touch you. When I began to realize how different this was, to test my theory I actually started to lean on the older gentleman in front of me at the bank. Ana was standing there too, and didn't even realize what I was doing until afterwards. I made it a joke with her, because at first I really had a hard time with my personal space being violated. Now I just take it in stride, but remain aware of the types of violations to make sure they are innocent. You are going to touch people; they are going to touch you. Just be certain they are not also reaching in your pocket and taking your wallet, cash, or phone.

<u>Driving Around Town</u>. I have already discussed the vendors and window washers in detail, so I won't belabor that point any further. I recommend you always keep your doors locked and your windows up as you drive around town. In most cities in the US this is standard practice. Over the years, I have had most of my vehicles programmed to lock the doors automatically when I put them in drive. If your car doors do not lock themselves, make it a habit to lock them when you start to drive. There is really not much to worry about, but it is one extra level of safety. I also want to mention how much tinting the windows on our car protected me from getting tickets. As soon as we had really dark windows, it was as if I had suddenly become Dominican. The street vendors don't try to sell me roses as much. The police don't even look at me any more. It's as if I just covered up the target.

If you get your own car, tint the windows. I don't know of any downside to this advice.

Events. I have been to many large events in the Dominican Republic, and have always been impressed with the level of security. They seem aware and very proactive. Other than the length of the lines and the chaos of trying to keep people in order, the event planners typically show their experience with preventative security measures. Events I have attended include New Years' parties, Carnival festivals, races, and concerts. I have also been to public functions on the *Malecon* and in the Colonial District. Most events have a lot of security guards at the entrance of the event, patting people down for guns. That is a great deterrent to keep some drunken idiot from shooting his gun in the air in celebration. I might add that I have seen people shoot guns in the air at the New Year. I don't know how to advise you on this matter, except to tell you to try to stay indoors as much as possible, and hope you are in one of the places with a foot-thick concrete ceiling. If you are in a home with a tin roof you will just have to pray the stray bullets go elsewhere.

The only time I really was freaked out at a public event was a *Raggetone* concert I attended with my wife, nieces and nephews. I don't know what happened to cause the audience to stampede; but suddenly they were running madly from one side of the stadium to the other. Kids were getting run over. Many ladies had fallen down. If you were near a fence or wall, you risked getting smashed by the masses. When the stampeding started, we immediately gathered everyone up and left. I don't know how that fiasco ended, but I am glad we were located near the exit. We made our way outside quickly.

Safety is more important to me than seeing some dude jump around on the stage while yelling into a microphone – I don't care who he is.

Travel by Car Around the Country. When you're driving around the country, be especially alert if you are driving at night. I have heard stories of people being stopped by police look-alikes and robbed. I have also heard of similar situations where a driver is caused to hit a person or some object, and then is pressured into giving money to stay out of jail or to avoid paying damages. I drive at night, but raise my level of caution. If I start feeling as if a particular car has been behind me for too long, I slow enough so they will pass. If a road block ahead appears to be unnecessary, I make sure there are several cars around before I go through it. Remember the rule of safety in numbers. I have not experienced any foul play myself, nor do I personally know anyone who has had problems while driving. I have friends and family who drive a lot at night. If you do drive at night, just be more cautious than you would during the day.

Airport Safety. The best advice for airport safety is to know the rules and follow them. In addition, I never get involved if there is something going on. It is not uncommon to see Dominicans yelling at the ticket agents. I let them do what they do; I just get my ticket and go. Do not carry unnecessary liquids, battery operated items, or weird electronics with you. Leaving unnecessary items at home makes getting through security easier. Also, once you arrive in the Dominican Republic, your lack of electronics is good because you have less to worry about. Just as when you are driving, when you're in the airport it's best always to be aware of your surroundings. Do not become a target by having excessive luggage or excessive jewelry. Always try to have plenty of time so you are not rushed. The more relaxed you are in traveling, the easier it will be for you to make rational decisions and to protect yourself and your belongings.

<u>Your Girlfriend or Wife.</u> I often read on message boards how tough tourist men will do something terrible to any Dominican they see staring at their wife or girlfriend. I have never seen the wives or girlfriends of these gentlemen; but I can't help wondering whether they really have anything to worry about! If they are that protective of the ladies, maybe they shouldn't leave their house. Although I've advised you many times to be aware of your surroundings, it's not necessary to be so aware that you are bothered by someone looking at you. It is culturally acceptable in the Dominican Republic for men to stare at a beautiful woman. In fact, I think there is a sort of Dominican pride for a man to know his lady is being looked over. They are proud to be the guy with the sexy woman.

Dominican men are very forward with the things they say to women. The almost automatic way to greet a woman is "my love," with "beautiful" or "cutie" coming in a very close second and third. There is, of course, a line, and I believe for the most part Dominican men know not to cross it. If your girl is taken, don't worry about the Dominican men. They won't even notice her. However, if she's available, then they will surely speak up. Women have an inherent way of telling men whether they are available or not. I'm not exactly sure what it is, but they just do. Don't worry. If your lady is cute, guys will notice. When you see someone checking out your wife or girlfriend, put your arm around her and smile at the guy. You'll get a grin back and that will be the end of it. There are way too many hot, beautiful, and sexy women running around this country for any Dominican man to be bothered too much about one woman who is already taken.

Women need to behave differently with regard to safety; but this is often the case, no matter where you live in the world. My wife is Dominican, so she already knows most of the rules. She knows a man with a gun will do bad things. Should she find herself in a situation with such a man, she knows she should do just about anything rather than going somewhere with him, where she would have no control. She feels it's better either to try to run, or to do her best to fight in a place where she is likely to get help.

Ana knows better than to tell anyone she is alone during the weeks I am away. She always says I will be back soon, but she isn't sure exactly when. Women have to be able to master the art of using unknowns to their advantage. They need to be able to act very calm in stressful situations, and they need to be able to keep their head about them if something starts to happen. When Ana and I first started dating, she had an experience where her quick wits saved her. She was leaving a friend's house late one night. She noticed the watchman sitting in his usual place, but was unable to tell if he was awake or asleep. Instead of speaking to him to make sure, she decided it was all right to go to her car. As she was getting into her car, a man with a gun said he was going to take her. Ana immediately went into defense mode. She told him she would be happy to take him wherever he wanted. It didn't seem possible to warn or get the attention of the watchman who was sitting in front of her friend's house. Almost instantaneously, she had to decide which was the better chance of escape: to run, or to try to make a getaway in the car.

She decided the best thing to do would be to act totally compliant, and to catch the guy off guard. He had been drinking heavily, and wasn't really able keep a constant eye on her. Very meekly, she said that she needed to get in her car to open the passenger door, because the lock on that side was broken. Talk about quick thinking! She looked wide-eyed and innocent, and she must have been convincing. The guy said, "Remember, I have a gun, and I'll shoot you if you try to get away." "I know," said Ana. "I just need to get into the car to unlock the door for you." As she slid into the driver's seat, she used one hand to lock the door behind her, while the other hand released the lock on the steering wheel. Then she pretended to reach across to the passenger door – but as she was leaning over, she started the car and drove off. She assumed the attacker would shoot, so she tried not to sit up, as she normally would while driving. She drove very fast to the corner, turned, and made her escape.

In my opinion, Ana was lucky the guy didn't open fire. She told me she would rather have him try to shoot her than take her hostage. She figured as soon as he started shooting, the watchman would realize what was going on, and he would start shooting too. Ana thought fast, choosing an action that would end the confrontation as quickly as possible, and with the least possible risk.

Think fast, if you find yourself in a similar situation. And don't second-guess yourself, once you've decided on a course of action. If you are being robbed, throw your money and your purse in two different directions, throw your phone in a third, and then run as if the devil were after you. Nothing material is worth injury.

Now that we're married, my wife wears a diamond ring. We've decided together that if anyone even looks at it, she is to give it to them. Ana knows the ring is worth a lot of money to some people; but she also knows it's worth nothing if she gets hurt trying to protect it. She will use it as a deterrent, if necessary, and will gladly throw the ring behind the attacker so that he'll turn around. She knows the ring is a symbol, but also that it is worthless in comparison to her safety.

If you're going to wear valuables, you need to know when to put them away and when it is time to use them to bargain. Oftentimes, an attacker will gladly take the jewels and go away. They really don't want the added risk of taking a hostage. A hostage ups the stakes considerably, and makes it much more likely that the ordeal will end with someone dying. Give them the easy money and let them go.

<u>Your House</u>. To protect your house, you just need to make sure you lock the door, even if you are only running out for a few minutes. I think having an alarm is a good safety precaution if you are going to be alone a lot. It will give you that added sense of security, knowing someone will call you if the alarm goes off. I also think steel window bars and a steel door are good safety precautions. We have them. After living behind bars for a while, I'm used to them. My wife's brother Tono is a contact for our alarm, in case it goes off when we are away from home; he is the only person who has a key to our house. We let our housekeeper into the house in the morning, when

we're at home; and when she leaves in the afternoon, one of us always is there to let her out. She never enters or leaves the house unattended. That will probably change, once we have children. We'll need someone to live in the house, take care of the children, and do shopping and run errands for us.

<u>Your Car</u>. I don't know if I need to say this, but you should lock your car. In Idaho, I used to leave the keys in the ignition and the windows down on my truck for months at a time. In Santo Domingo, I don't go into the market without locking and putting one of those steering wheel locks on the car. I don't know anyone who has had a car stolen, but I have read of such problems online.

One thing I would suggest is to take your car to a service station that installs locking lug nuts. This makes it a little harder to steal your tires and hub caps. I think the reality is, if someone wants your car badly enough, they are going to get it. If they want to steal parts from your car, they are going to steal the parts. Just try to make it a little harder for them to steal your parts than parts from the car parked next to you, and you'll probably get passed over.

Our spare tire and tire cover were stolen one night, right in front of the cake store. It happened in about two minutes. The watchman outside claimed that he was eating, and didn't see anything. I think the robbers gave him food, and in exchange, he told them the coast was clear. I was inside the store, less than twenty feet away, walking around in front of the window. We had insurance, so it ended up costing us only about two thousand *pesos*. Since then, we have had locking lugs put on all the tires, and we have a locking mechanism on our spare.

I do know of one person who had all four tires

stolen while she was inside a friend's house. She came out to find her car sitting right on the road where she left it, but without the tires. To me, having something stolen every now and then is just part of life, no matter where you live. We also had the rear-view mirror stolen off the driver's side of our car while we were visiting a friend in the hospital, right in the middle of the day. I think that cost US$100. Since these two incidents, I make it a point to greet the guardians courteously, and I try to park close to where they are sitting. If they are close to my car and nothing is missing when I return, I give them twenty or thirty *pesos*. If they are not there, or they come running over from far away when I return, I give them ten *pesos*. I also tell them they need to stay closer to my car next time, or I won't pay them. Sometimes I get in the car and drive off without their even noticing. That means they are not paying close enough attention to warrant any payment at all. I just leave the change in the cup I keep in the jockey box for the next time I need to pay a watchman.

Valuables in Your Home when You Have House Help. Dominicans hide valuables in the weirdest of places! My wife is so good at hiding money that even she can never find it. Every now and then she will open a book, or box, or drawer and find some money. It is rather like an Easter egg hunt. In my opinion, this is the wrong way to protect valuables. Ana and I have a different approach to protecting our valuables. To begin with, we have very few valuable belongings, so it is not tough for us to protect them. Second, the valuables we do have are not necessarily hidden so that they are hard to find. They are hidden to avoid the attention of the housekeeper and visitors. For example, my passport is kept in a cover, and hidden either in the bottom pair of jeans in my pile of jeans, or in the inside pocket of my suitcase, which is left sitting open in the closet. There is no reason for anyone to look in my suitcase, and it is very unlikely our housekeeper will unfold the bottom pair of jeans. It's hard enough to get her to fold and put away the ones she just washed, let alone restacking or refolding ones already in the closet.

We are looking into the possibility of putting a small safe in the house. My wife feels that a safe is just a signpost, to let everyone know where all the valuables are. I believe a properly-hidden safe will not only be a little more secure, but also a place where all the things Ana "hides" can be kept without risk of losing them forever. I will probably buy the safe and install it by myself. We have several ideas for where it can be mounted and hidden in places not commonly thought of, yet easy enough to access that it won't hinder its use on a regular basis. We'll see…

<u>Do Not Get Hurt: and If You Do, What Next?</u> During the time I have been in the DR, two of my close friends have been very severely injured. One, Ricardo, was injured at work when he was adjusting something on a generator. He was shocked so badly that the entry wounds of the electricity burned the skin completely off one arm, and the exit blew a grapefruit-sized hole in his knee. He probably should have died but Ricardo is in very good shape, and even refused to lie down during or after the incident. He actually made the ambulance drive in front of him while he ran part-way to the hospital. His theory was that as long as his heart kept beating, he was alive. I have no idea if his theory is correct, but it worked; so

if I'm ever in the same position, I'm going to follow the same instructions.

I am not telling you this story to convince you that you should run after being shocked. In fact, I have no idea if that was good advice, or advice that will kill you if you're not as strong and healthy as Ricardo. The point I'm making is that he was taken to a very nice private hospital in the capital and was given top medical care. He stayed in a private room, cared for by what appeared to be top doctors, nurses, and medical staff. They applied some sort of synthetic skin that ended up grafting and growing along with his skin. Right now, about six months after the injury, he has some red scars that will eventually be hardly noticeable. I believe the medical attention Ricardo received was probably equivalent to the care one would receive in a good US hospital, but with the luxury of having a private room.

Now let me tell you about my other friend, Manolo. He was at a New Year's Eve party, which I did not personally attend; so I don't know what kind of party it was. Let's just assume it was a get-together of people in front of the local *colmado*, so the setting is easy to envision. (Note: a *colmado* is a sort of convenience store, like a 7/11, but with the added service of delivery.) One thing led to another throughout the night. There was the usual music, and a crowd was gathered, happily drinking and dancing. Everyone was enjoying the evening. At just after midnight, one extremely drunk individual decided he would break a bottle to celebrate, and then swing the bottle around. No one knows why he did this, or even if he knew what he was doing. In an attempt to move people out of the way or stop this guy, Manolo ended up getting the bottle stuck on the inside of his arm, just at his elbow. The next day, after the bottle and all the glass shards were removed from his arm, we could see that the cut was about six inches long and looked to me to be about two inches deep. I don't know how it did not cut the main artery running on the soft inside of his arm.

Manolo, being fairly intoxicated himself that night, decided he would just wrap the cut up and go home to bed. In my opinion, he is lucky he woke up in the morning. By the time I saw him at around 10:00 the next morning, when he arrived at my in-laws' house, he looked very sick. I could tell from about ten yards away he was not doing well. In fact, he looked so awful that I wondered how he was continuing to walk. He was very pale, and his skin looked cold. He looked weak and just barely conscious. Fortunately, Manolo is a pretty big guy and fairly strong, so he was able to handle a lot more pain than a smaller person could. When we saw the blood that was still running down his arm from under the bandage, we immediately rushed him to the emergency room.

Now, the difference between this story and Ricardo's story is that Manolo does not have a great-paying job. He has no insurance, and definitely does not have money to pay for a private hospital. I drove him to the closest emergency room. (We stopped at a clinic on the way, but it was closed).

This was a public emergency room in a public hospital. This is where everyone without money or insurance who had been wounded, injured, or broken on New Year's Eve was taken. The place was a madhouse. All things considered, I feel the staff did an amazing job; but it was a mess. The building was a single-floor cinderblock construction with a bare concrete floor. Most walls either were not painted, or were painted the same grey as the cinderblock. There was no glass in the windows. There were bars for security purposes, with expanded steel for further reinforcement behind the bars. To allow for air flow, shutters were open.

The main waiting room contained about twenty chairs and three observation and operating rooms. Each room was packed with victims. Immediately inside the main entrance on the right was a room reserved for everyone who was injured but not bleeding. I saw roughly thirty people in that room when we arrived – standing room only.

Just past that room on the opposite side of the hall was the Men's Trauma Center. The Men's Trauma Center was reserved for those who had severe breaks or cuts, and were at risk of losing limbs or even worse, their lives. This room had two beds where patients lay while they were being operated on, and a long counter against the far wall under the windows. Our friend was bleeding and at risk of losing his arm, or possibly worse. We entered the Men's Trauma Center.

Two doctors were busily stitching up victims who lay on the operating tables. On the far side of the room, three nurses or assistants were working on patients lying on the counter under the window. Another doctor, immediately to my right, was sewing the remainder of a hand on one poor fellow who was half sitting on the table, half lying against the wall. I could hardly believe it: there were pools of blood on the floor, probably several cupfuls. Several cups of blood are a LOT! If you don't agree, go to your kitchen and get a cup, fill it up with water, and pour it on the floor. From the way the blood was splattered all over the floor, I guessed it was from four or five different victims who had previously been here. The fellow with the partial hand only had a little blood on the floor under where he was sitting.

The other doctor, who was to my left, was diligently replacing the skin on some gentleman's heel. It looked as if the gentleman were riding a *moto* and then, as he hit forty miles an hour, shoved his bare foot in the back spokes of the *moto* in an attempt to stop. I could see tendons, veins, muscle, bone, and if I knew any other anatomy words I'd throw them in too. It was gross. When we entered, the second doctor, the one closest to the door and to the left, looked up and smiled: apparently, Manolo was his cousin. Man, some days it's really good to have a lot of relatives! The doctor immediately stopped what he was doing to take a quick look at Manolo's wound. He told my friend to sit at the other end of the table where he was working and he'd take care of him next. Ana is such an awesome girl – she went in and held my friend's hand. Manolo's is actually her cousin, and she wanted to help him through this. As they entered the room she smartly closed the door and propped a chair in front of it so no one else would come wandering in and bother the doctor.

After a few minutes in the room trying to comfort Manolo, I started feeling really claustrophobic. All the people, the several simultaneous surgeries, the smell, the blood, the pain and anguish – it was all just too much for me to handle. I needed to get some fresh air. Unfortunately, I had just thrown on a pair of sandals for the trip to the hospital. I kept imagining that the blood lying in puddles on the floor would just jump over the side of my sandal and onto my foot. This fear was compounded as I walked around the corner to see what was happening in Room Three – and stepped on a discarded syringe tip. It was uncovered and looked as if it had been used. Now, it only stuck into my sandal, but in my mind it did much more. I visualized it sticking through the sandal and into my foot. I had had enough! As I pushed my way down the hall to the exit door, I noticed the third room was equally packed. This place was just too much for me.

The point of telling you these two stories is to emphasize that if you are injured in the DR, make sure you go to a private hospital. My wife has strict orders that if I am injured and cannot last long enough for a flight to Miami, I am to go to a private hospital. I'm sure you understand why!

What Would I Do Differently?

People often ask me if I am happy in my new home. I think you can tell from reading this that yes, in fact, I am very happy. However, I would do some things differently, were I to go about this again. Here are the top things I would do differently:

Get Serious about Spanish. One of the stupidest things I have done is not take advantage of all the people who would be more than happy to help me work on my Spanish. I have gone to classes here and there; but other than one stretch for about eight months where I went three times a week, I really never got serious about learning Spanish. It could be that I am a slow learner and cannot pick up a new language on my own. At any rate, I have never switched to speaking only Spanish. I still struggle in conversations.

Here's what I should have done. First, I should have enrolled in classes at Dominico Americano, or another Spanish school, and just forced myself to go. Even if I missed two weeks a month because of my travel schedule, I would have learned loads more Spanish, and would have become more confident faster.

Second, I should have gotten Ana to help me more with learning her first language. I don't know why, but we only speak together in English. I did not even know one word of Spanish when I first came here; so she has had to translate for me for most of the time I have been here. I am pretty easy to entertain, so in a crowd, I can usually find someone who will speak English. When that doesn't happen, I can follow most conversations for a long time. I don't know how to get your wife to help you learn the language: it hasn't worked for me.

One of the funniest things I have done as I have been learning Spanish was to think my construction skills from the US will work here. Doesn't it make sense to expect to go to the hardware store and buy things, because everything is labeled in English and you can just walk around until you find what you want? Well, not exactly. One day I went to find the blinds for our bedroom windows. We needed three different mini-blinds, but decided to get one, and I would install it in the master bedroom. If we liked it, I would go and buy the same ones for the other windows.

I went to the store and bought a single blind, which seemed perfect. It was the exact size and color we needed. The box looked as if someone had opened it to show it to a buyer, but they obviously did not want it because it was still here. The store realized the box was opened, so they had reduced the price. I had lived in the DR long enough to know that it is common to buy things that have already been opened. I was actually a little happy because it was discounted. At the time, I felt the blinds were very expensive compared to the prices I was used to seeing in the States; so I was happy to buy the one that was opened, and save a few bucks.

I noticed "DANADO" written in marker on the side of the box. I thought, "That's great! They have already marked it to let the cashier know it's less expensive because it was opened." When I got to the checkout counter, I told the lady I had talked to the guy working with the blinds and he told me I would get a discount. She shrugged and looked at me as if to say, "Well, if he promised you a discount on this thing, I guess I'll give it to you." I started dreaming up ways I could go home and install this blind, then come back with the receipt and see if they would match the discount. Maybe I could talk them into a closeout special. This was going to be great! Ana was going to love the color, and I was going to install the blind perfectly.

I got home, measured the holes, and drilled them in our concrete walls. I installed the mounts and installed the blind. This was even easier than I had thought it would be. I had measured everything perfectly; it was squared; it was leveled. It was perfect! As I let the draw-cord down to allow the blind to cover the window for the first time – the whole bottom of the blind fell completely to the floor. The damn thing was BROKEN! Who the hell did they think they were, selling me a broken blind?

I immediately called my wife. I was irate. She said she would help me take it back, and would look at it with me when she came home that evening. I spent the rest of the afternoon thinking about how much I wanted to call the store and yell. I was ready to go off the handle: *Sell me some broken piece of crap? What are you _thinking_!*

When Ana got home around 7:00, she said the installation job looked perfect. It would be just fine: all we needed to do was to take this one back and get another one. She asked for the receipt, and asked how I negotiated a discount. I proudly told her that I had negotiated the discount because the box had been opened. They had used this one for a display. Then I announced that I thought I could negotiate the other ones for the same price. What an idiot! At almost exactly the same moment, my wife grabbed me, laughing so hard she had tears running down her cheeks. She hugged me, crying and laughing, pointing at the box lying in the corner. She laughed so hard she couldn't talk. All she could do was go get a dictionary and open it to DANADO: "broken."

Just in case you're wondering, NO, I was not able to negotiate the same discount on the other two blinds I needed. I was happy to pay full price for ones in boxes that had not even been looked at before. I actually inspected them to make sure they were unopened. The lesson here is – Learn Spanish.

Stop Using Air Conditioning Sooner. The last places I lived in the United States were Northern Idaho, Utah, and Washington DC. Each of these places experiences several months each year where the weather seldom gets above freezing. In fact, in Northern Idaho there are times when the sun only comes up for a couple of hours each day – not even long enough to thaw something out. These climates gave me the ability to withstand severe cold. I could walk outside in the winter barefoot, in shorts, and with no shirt, just to get the paper or to get the mail. While these temperatures were nothing to me, they would probably kill or seriously injure most Dominicans.

When I came to the Dominican Republic, my body thought I had gone from heaven to hell. It was like being stuck in a sauna with the steam and heat turned all the way up. I only had to look outside and my body would turn on the sweat glands. Any time I left an air-conditioned area for more than one second, my shirt would be dripping wet. It was so ridiculous – Ana would carry napkins in her purse to wipe the sweat off my forehead, cheeks, and neck. For me, it was a miserable adjustment. I had problems with sweat in all the places you just do not want problems with sweat. I always had to air myself out when I got back to my hotel room.

My initial reaction was to try to counteract the heat by keeping my air conditioning cranked up to maximum cold. It would give me goose bumps when I first walked into my room after I'd been running. I think I even remember one day when I could see steam rising off my body as I happily stood in front of the air-conditioning vent. The problem was that I wasn't always in a place with air conditioning. We would often go to Ana's family's house, where they have fans (as long as there is power). When there was no power, the fans would stop working. I used to take three shirts for each day when we were going to be at her parents' house. I changed my undershirt and my top shirt three times each day. You are probably wondering, "Hey. genius, if you sweat so much, why were you wearing two shirts?" Good point. Well, I had to resort to masking the sweat by wearing two shirts rather than just one; with only one shirt, I was dripping in no time. Besides, if I wore an undershirt and then a shirt to cover the sweaty one, I looked more Dominican (remember the discussion of this above), and I didn't look as if I was dying of heat.

We noticed an interesting phenomenon when we moved into our new house. Our house has ceiling fans throughout. We installed an air conditioning unit in our bedroom so I could at least sleep in peace. For the first three months, I froze my wife out. Ana would cover herself with all the blankets, and I would happily lie there in my underwear, shirtless, and soak up the wonderfully cold air. It was just like being back in heaven. The phenomenon happened after I fell asleep each night. My wife decided I had had enough heaven. She turned off the air conditioning about an hour after I had fallen asleep. She then ditched the blankets, and we both woke up happy and comfortable. At first, there were a couple of days when I woke up sweating and turned on the air conditioning, but for the most part, I wasn't really bothered.

Eventually we decided I was sleeping well enough that we should just set the timer on the air conditioner. It would give me an hour to crash, and then it would turn off on its own. This would allow Ana to sleep the whole night and not have to wake up to turn off heaven. I first observed the phenomenon one movie night (the night my wife watches girly sitcoms and I just hang out, or go to bed early) when I actually fell asleep without the air conditioning, and slept the whole night. The next night Ana reminded me I had slept without heaven the night before; since I was getting used to it, she thought I should just see if I could do without the air conditioning. The amazing thing was – I slept perfectly.

We keep our ceiling fan on so the air is moving well, but I haven't used the air conditioning much since. I have found that since I stopped using the air conditioning I sweat less. I don't sweat like I used to when we're sitting in the living room. I don't drip sweat on my computer in my office. I don't sweat when I walk down the front hall toward where heaven is located. It is a phenomenon I cannot explain. Now I'm going to share something so weird that I haven't told Ana yet; she'll be shocked if she ever reads this. There have been a few times this winter when I purposely pulled our sheet over my feet because they were cold. I think that living here has ruined my ability to function properly in the winter.   If I ever go back to Moscow I'll probably die…

<u>Plan Better to Stop Traveling</u>.   One of the problems of having a well-paying job is that you get comfortable with the money. You learn to deal with the stresses and inconvenience the traveling causes. My job required me to travel every Sunday, which meant I missed a lot of weekend trips. I also missed out on family events and most holidays. I was able to justify this by looking at the deposits I would receive in my bank account twice each month.

I knew that job would not last forever; nothing does, especially nowadays, with the way the entire world has become infatuated with outsourcing, right-sizing, and downsizing. This uncertainty is only compounded by the current economic fiasco.   I'll talk about this in much greater detail in the section below, titled "Potential Jobs and Income Sources." I just wish I had done a better job of maximizing my secondary income sources, so when it was my turn to be downsized it wouldn't have been so much of a shock. In the end, things will work out fine. They always seem to. It would just have been less stressful to know I had an extra two thousand or so coming in each month with very little to no effort.

<u>International Calling on Your Cell Phone</u>. I learned very quickly that using my US cell phone while I was in the Dominican Republic was very expensive. It was not uncommon for me to have a cell phone bill of two to three hundred dollars each month just because I used my cell phone in the DR as if I were living in the US. It seems to me that Dominicans talk much less on the phone than Americans do. I may be incorrect with this generalization; but many Dominicans get by with a cell phone plan of 150, 300, or even 500 minutes each month. They don't know about plans that offer 1000 minutes. They have never even heard of a plan with unlimited minutes. They just don't spend the time on the phone we Americans do.

After a few months of paying the extra fees for roaming, I just turned off my US cell phone each week that I was in the DR. I left a voice message that I was traveling and it would be easier to reach me by email; and I gave my email address. This cut way down on the amount of time I spent on the phone. I got only one or two emails a week at first; but I slowly trained people not to call me. I purchased a prepaid Dominican cell phone for around ten bucks, and I buy minutes. If people in the US really need to reach me, they can either call my US cell, which now rings through on my computer, or they can spend the money to call my Dominican cell phone. It is up to them. I probably could have saved several thousand dollars if I had purchased the Dominican cell phone on the first trip; but I guess that's where experience comes in. One nice thing about the Dominican calling plans is that they charge the same to talk to someone in the Dominican Republic as they do to call someone in the US.

<u>Want to Take the Plunge?</u>

If you are still reading, you may be interested in moving to the Dominican Republic. Would you like to know what it really takes to pull off this move? If you are planning on moving or spending extended time in the Dominican Republic, this section will probably be the most important section in the whole book for you. Here I'm going to talk about the two "elephants in the room"— the Mentality and Money. You can actually narrow that down to just one elephant – Money. If you have enough money, you can accommodate your mentality to the situation. I'll discuss Mentality first, and then Money.

<u>What It Takes Mentally</u>. When you decide it is time to take the plunge you need to ask yourself why? Why do you want to move to the Dominican Republic? Why now? What do you hope to gain from the experience? Are you trying to get away from something? Is the Dominican weather your reason for wanting to move? What are you looking for? As you start to define what you are hoping to find with this move, you need to build in safeguards against discouragement. You may even need to consider whether you should wait or prepare better before you take the leap.

When I first decided I was going to move, my best friend Jon and his wife Janae told me there would be a day when I wondered what I had been thinking when I made that decision. They wanted me to call them when that day came, so they could talk me through it. At the time I thought there was no way this would ever happen. But it did happen, and more than once.

The reality is that life is not perfect, no matter where you live. If you're running away from problems, you'll find the DR has problems of its own. If you're running toward Paradise, you'll find that Paradise comes with electricity issues, mosquitoes, and a host of other delightful details. Just remember why you decided to move in the first place, and try to keep that in the forefront of your mind.

Earlier, I mentioned that I always try to think about the positive aspects of Dominican life when I feel discouraged. I have already written about many differences in lifestyle that can make your transition tough. In this section, I'll deal with potential problems for which you need to be mentally prepared. You may not need to worry about some of these issues if your finances are in good order.

For me, one of the biggest mental challenges was coping with the stress and pressure from my job. I was making my living as a full-time salesperson, traveling from city to city selling software. Pressures for me were based on needing to keep my numbers up. I had to interact with many different managers and other individuals who seemed to think I got better treatment because of my different living conditions. I had to travel every Sunday, with my last flight often landing late at night. When I was headed to work, I would then have to rent a car and drive to my hotel – at times, several hours away.

In my high-pressure position, performance was only one of the requirements for keeping the job. Besides the need to be a top performer, there were major political aspects to keeping managers and other office higher-ups happy. I'm good at selling, but not so good with office politics. As a result, I often got tough rotations, and was put with teams that needed closing or sales skill, but that had difficult markets. The job was a constant struggle. I would report to work each week already counting the days until I was able to return to Paradise. I never lost count. There were times I paid extra money to get an early flight out Saturday night. To me, getting away from work and heading to Paradise was worth the extra cost. My job was not secure and was threatened week to week, but it was all I had, and it made it possible for me to live in the DR, for which I was grateful.

On top of the constant pressure of just doing the job, traveling also presented me with a lot of stress. More than once, my managers warned me if I ever missed a flight or missed a connection, or was delayed enough to miss a day of work, I would no longer be able to fly out of the Dominican Republic, and I could lose my job. This caused me to be ever more vigilant in making sure I never missed a day of work. I did miss flights. I did miss connections. I even had flights completely canceled. Considering all that, in the four years I traveled to and from work from the Dominican Republic, *I never missed even one day of work*! I was late to a couple of events because of unfortunate late night cancellations; but I never missed a full day of work.

I began to carry clothes in my carry-on, so if my bag did not make it, I always had a set of clothing to wear to work the next day. I also became accustomed to sleeping in the airport and on the planes, so I could be prepared for an unexpected all-night drive. I have made more all-night drives during my four years traveling out of the Dominican Republic than I have my entire life. They just seemed to happen.

The travel became manageable. Not knowing

exactly where I would sleep on any given night didn't bother me. I could usually find a hotel and check in with no effort. I could sleep in a chair at the airport or on the flight, no problem. The issues that simply drove me crazy had to do with weather. No one controls the weather. Unfortunately, I was in a position where I had to be on top of things so I didn't miss work because of the weather. I scheduled my trips around several hurricanes. I have spent a few extra days holed up in a random city because of airport closures due to snow, sleet, and ice. I learned to watch the radar weather and to plan for my way out of the Dominican Republic if a storm should suddenly change course. The weather was the worst stress.

Also stressful for me were the constant flight delays that seemed to plague the airlines. I have sat on a tarmac at an airport for hours, waiting for a gate to open. While we sat, my next flight left. I've spent countless hours waiting for the door of the airplane to be closed due to some maintenance problem; or even worse, endless hours waiting on the plane after the door has been shut! Nothing about the airlines and their poor management of maintenance, scheduling of gates, cancellation of flights, or changes of flight times made my life easy. The airlines were simply an enemy I had to deal with. If you are going to fly weekly, get used to the airlines and their issues, because you will truly be at their mercy.

I always tried to have a plan and also a back-up plan for each of my travel weeks. If my main flight got canceled, I would have a secondary flight in mind. If I missed the last connection, I would have a plan for other ways to get to my hotel. Would I be able to drive in at night and still make it for my first meeting the next morning? Would I need to get a cab to drive me?

What about a train or other methods of transportation? Planning, organization and preparation are the keys to lowering stress. It was amazing how many times I used my back-up plan, which often worked out better than the original plan.

I said earlier that you should make a list of things you love about the Dominican Republic and remind yourself of them each time you have doubts. Well, that is absolutely the best approach to every problem or situation. Remember that there are just as many problems or issues everywhere else. The Dominican Republic has less of some issues and more of others. Remember why you love it here, and you'll make it!

<u>Money.</u> The truth is, there is a whole lot more money to be made each year than a six-figure income. Top salespeople make seven figures each year. Consultants, specialists, and other professionals can command even higher incomes. If you have the ability, use it! Make sure you are earning what you are worth, and always perform above expectations. Each of us has to determine what our earning threshold is, and then figure out what we need to do to get there. For some it will be easy. For others, the task will be daunting.

During my time in the Dominican Republic, I have had the opportunity to meet people from several different industries who travel frequently in and out of the country. I'm going to tell you about a few career options and what kind of income can be expected from each. I believe having control over your income is the best way to make a living, but having a job with flexibility is also a big plus. In any case, try to plan ahead in case things change suddenly and your income stream disappears.

You really have two choices: you can either make your living from outside the country, meaning you travel or telecommute to work; or you can make your income from within the Dominican Republic. In my opinion, it's easier to make a higher wage by getting your income from outside the country, because first-world markets can support better incomes. In fact, it is not uncommon for someone to make six figures annually in the first- world markets.

Let's consider several job options for making your money outside of the Dominican Republic. The first possibility that comes to mind would be to get a job working for a seminar company. These jobs require the staff to travel from one location to the next; so management may be more likely to let you live where you want. Most positions with seminar companies are sales-related. Some background in sales is required for working with a seminar company

I know several attorneys and accountants who work part of the year in the United States and then spend the rest of the year in the DR. Their theory is, they make enough income during the months they work, so they can then take the rest of the year off. The idea here is to get a temp job or contract job where you work very intensively for a given period of time. Work like crazy: and then when you're done with the project, go to the DR to decompress. I have a close friend who does contract legal work and saves enough money to travel two to three months each year. Last year he went to Central America to study Spanish. This year he is headed to South America. The same concept would work well for someone who wanted to live in the DR.

One of my other friends works summers selling

alarm systems. His company sends him to a location and puts him up in an apartment for the summer. He works six or seven days a week for three months or so, and pulls in around a hundred thousand. Then he goes home to be with his family for the rest of the year. If your family can handle your absence for this length of time, go for it. It can be great money for those who have the ambition to sell.

Probably the most common jobs requiring consistent travel are jobs relating to consulting and sales. Many consultants are put on an assignment for months at a time, and are required to fly weekly to assist their clients. I have met consultants who travel weekly across the US, or even twice a month to Europe. Get the right consulting gig and you can live just about anywhere you want.

The Dominican Republic is unique because it has a concentration of great baseball players. Most of the major-league teams have schools or camps here, where they begin recruiting and training kids at very young ages. If you have a sports background, there's a ton of different positions related to sports and recruiting. I have a friend who flies two to three times each month to Santo Domingo to see how his team's school is doing. He is responsible for recruiting, and for the overall performance of the recruiting program. He lives in a nice hotel when he is here and he is taken care of very well. I have met countless others who are coaches, trainers, or managers of one sort or another. They scout out players. They come and watch teams and practices. They do whatever it is that the business side of the sports teams wants them to do. They make the business run. These individuals will be taken care of, and they can live pretty much wherever they want. I know of people who live all over the East Coast from north to south and all the way to Texas, who travel on a regular basis to the Dominican Republic. If sports are your thing, get into the business side of baseball. It seems to me there are plenty of opportunities for the right people.

One of the most versatile, yet specific, roles a person can play for a living is being a freelance writer. There are people who make their living writing books, articles, and even blogging on the Internet. If you have the ability to write well, think about people you know who might like to have you write for them. Start to research on the Internet for possible positions as a writer, editor, or publisher. Write some articles and publish them to get started. Look for writing competitions. Find people or companies who are willing to pay you to write for them. Companies are always looking for people who can write their product reviews. They need handbooks and manuals, direct-mail pieces and sales letters. Companies need so many different things written, and many of them are happy to hire freelancers to write for them. The key is to be on the lookout for them as they come up.

Let's switch gears now and discuss the many different ways to make a living from within the Dominican Republic. I have to caution you first: don't think it will be easy for you to find a position that will pay you a living wage. Most Dominicans do not live in a household with only one income earner. Most Dominican families have several individuals working and pitching in to help make ends meet. Otherwise, Dominicans often do not make enough to live. As a foreigner, you'll be at a disadvantage because you don't speak the language as well as the locals. You won't be as connected with people who know about good positions, and you won't be accustomed to the working environment. Dominicans work very long hours!

Just because you think you notice Dominicans taking long lunches and frequent breaks, don't be misled into thinking they do not work. Many Dominicans do the work two people would do in North America. They may not be as efficient, but they do work long hours. You won't see overtime pay after eight hours, and you will not have many of the rights to which you were accustomed in the first world. In addition, Dominicans are happy to work for much less than you or I would consider "survival pay". My wife makes about 20% of what someone makes in the US doing the equivalent job. She is very well-educated and works very long hours; she just makes less. She says she is well-paid because she makes a lot more than most people do. It is just a different mind-set.

If you are going to move to the Dominican Republic and are not able to live on your savings, then I would recommend not trying to compete with Dominicans in their job market. It seems to me to be a losing scenario for most foreigners. There are a couple of exceptions. Because of your ability to read, write, and speak English, you can work in a call center. In this type of job, you can make more than the average Dominican; and in some cases, you can even make an almost- respectable income, depending on the job and whether there are commissions involved. The second exception would be if you have a good connection who can help you get a position that pays enough for you to call it a "living wage".

Otherwise, I would not recommend counting on any money from a local job. I believe the best opportunities for foreigners are to use the advantages they have. Exploit the opportunities you can manage, that wouldn't be open to most locals. For example, open a small business. It is a fact that there are more self-employed Dominicans than there are self- employed Americans. This is because most Dominicans realize they have the ability to control more when they are "the boss". They can work harder to make more money, and they can take time off if they want to. I believe many foreigners have the ability to open small businesses with which they can make the most of their advantages and make a fairly good living.

If you have experience as a quality-control person, open a small quality control firm. You can contract with companies to improve their quality standards. If you are an engineer or architect, become a consultant to engineers or architects on the proper advances in their technology. If you have any training whatsoever in technology, capitalize on it. Web designers, web developers, web marketers, graphics design: the list of possibilities could go on and on. Each of these areas has the potential of providing you and your family a great living. If you are a photographer, set yourself up to take pictures at weddings. Many weddings take place each year with the bride and groom not understanding much of what the photographer wants. Advertise to the English-speaking market while you learn Spanish. Once you are somewhat fluent in Spanish, use your ability to speak and otherwise communicate in English as a way to get paid. I believe being a consultant who teaches businesses a certain skill or strategy is one of the best ways to capitalize on your strengths. Put together a small consulting firm, and you're off.

I have been known to do a form of negotiation or selling for companies. A company contracts with me to negotiate on their behalf with their clients who are not fluent in Spanish. They give me a percentage of whatever business I bring in. For example, an exporter needs to sell some vegetables. They have a client in New York who would like to buy direct; but they have communications problems. I can step in and very quickly convince the client to place an order and make them comfortable dealing with the seller. I am just a voice on the phone, but a very skilled voice that can negotiate and sell.

I also know people who have web businesses. These individuals sell things they buy from other people; they make money when they sell at a higher price than they bought. This is the traditional business model, where the retail seller buys from a manufacturer or distributor and then sells to the public. The modern twist is that the seller never physically takes control of the product. They simply sell the product on their website, and the supplier ships the product directly to the buyer. This is a great way to make some money if you have the connections for the product. After you learn about drop shipping and affiliate marketing, the hardest part of this business is finding the right product to sell or the right supplier for the product you want to sell. I won't get into detail on this type of business because there are millions of places you can learn about it. Just be aware that a home business in a first-world country can be an income in the Dominican Republic.

When people visit the DR and consider becoming a resident, one of the first potential income sources that come to mind is becoming an exporter. They experience the fabulously delicious fruits and vegetables, and believe they themselves are going to take them to the rest of the world! Well, this is a great first idea; but as you begin to learn about this business, you'll discover how difficult it really is. As you go out driving around the countryside and visiting farms, if you pay attention you will see thousands of small trucks. Their owners, who are exporters, drive these small trucks. The bulk of the fruit-exporting business is tied up by big conglomerates, which contract with the farmers on their yearly crop yields. The majority of the Asian vegetable market is made up of thousands of small exporters. These are businesses that really work to make their money. I know first hand that a single container of produce takes many man-hours to prepare; and in the end, after the exporter pays labor and expenses, he only earns one hundred dollars in profit. Exporting is a very tough business. Oftentimes, the connections are where the money is made. The business of exporting a commodity is rife with risk: shipments go bad; boxes break; orders are late.

I am not trying to discourage you from venturing into exporting. I just think the best way to go about it is first to find the buyers, and then to approach the exporter. Your proposal should be that they will do the physical work and you will find the buyers. Remember that I advised you to capitalize on your strengths? Well, your strength is not picking fruit and vegetables. I don't care who you are: your strength in this situation will always be contacts or your language skills. Use your strengths.

A final option I will discuss for making an income in the Dominican Republic is teaching. Many foreigners make a living teaching English or other skills. If you have a particular skill and can put a class together, do it. Best of all, if you are a teacher in your home country, by all means try to teach here. If you go to work for a school, you won't make more than around two hundred dollars each month. Being a private tutor allows you to control your rate of pay by charging per client and per hour. Advertise your teaching skill, and find a few good clients who will pay you for your skill. This will enable

you to make as much in a week as you would have in a
month with a "job". You may even be able to charge your
clients in dollars.

When the subject of living and making money
in the Dominican Republic comes up, People often ask
me whether I pay taxes. I have always paid taxes in the
United States because I have never been able to stay
outside of the country long enough to make the foreign
earned income exemption. In order to qualify, you need
to be outside of the United States for eleven months a
year. If you are in the US for more than thirty days out
of the year, you won't meet the exemption. I am hoping
to change that one day by not going into the US for an
entire year. That way, I'll be able get the advantage of
the $75,000 income without having to pay United States
taxes. We'll see how that goes, particularly in the current
tax strapped economy.

Making your living in the Dominican Republic
will require you to adjust your thinking from the fast-
paced, money-driven perspective to a more relaxed,
make-ends-meet-while-you- enjoy-life mentality. After
all, if you are living in the Dominican Republic, you are
in one of the most beautiful countries on the planet and
living among some of the happiest people on the earth.
Live your life to the fullest, and don't forget to enjoy all
the small things.

The Last Chapter

In preparing this book, I have considered all the aspects of life in the Dominican Republic that struck me as odd, or that were difficult for me to deal with. I tried to be as open as possible, and to "tell it like it is".

Now that I have done that, let me be a little more open with you about me. I have become so enamored with the Dominican Republic that Ana and I plan to raise our children here. We would like to have them attend elementary school in the United States for a year or two; and then we are going to persuade them to attend college or university in the United States.

I absolutely love the Dominican lifestyle and feel there is much less stress and pressure in the Dominican Republic than in the United States. What's best about the country is that the people are able to do what they want, as long as they are not hurting others too much. There are very few lawsuits where people sue other people for millions of dollars because they fell down. Most of the year the weather is gorgeous; and the times when you have to stay indoors because of a storm are opportunities to become really close with your family.

Every Dominican I have ever met is proud of being Dominican. It makes no difference whether they were born in the USA or in the DR. Dominicans love their heritage, and are proud to show it. Dominicans understand that life is not perfect. They meet problems like power outages, shortages of gas, and adjusting their schedules at the last minute with equanimity – and because of that they are happier than most North Americans. I love seeing someone who has literally nothing sit and talk about how good life has been to them, just because they are happy. It is amazing. I wish most first-world countries could teach their citizens to live life with this kind of joy.

As I have written this book, the world has entered one of the most severe economic crises in history. Many of my friends and family have lost their jobs. I have seen the devastation American families suffer due to reduced financial means, but I have only seen my wife and her family be ever more supportive. When I faced a time where my traveling sales job was put on hold, Ana was not upset: she said it was exciting to have a new opportunity. I am lucky to have a Dominican wife who lives life to its fullest and is happy. I have friends who have lost their jobs, who are also headed toward losing houses; the pressure of it is causing them to experience a significant amount of stress in their family lives. My Dominican family told me I had worked too hard for too long, and now I needed to take a three-month vacation. What an eye-opening society! To live because you love life, not because you need to acquire more and more, is the lesson the *Republica Dominicana* has taught me.

If you have read this book and are thinking of moving, my advice is to plan – and then to do it. You never know what is over the horizon. My current lifestyle is much better than I had ever dreamed of. I wake up in the morning and make breakfast for my wife, as she gets ready for work. I then check emails and do business for a couple hours, as needed. Mid-morning, I head out for a run round town. I usually run for between an hour and an hour and a half each day. It is my own time and I love it! I have been on almost every street in the Capital and can't wait to go out and explore tomorrow! Ana and I eat lunch at around 1:00 each day. Some days we eat at our house; others we go out to eat or join the family. In the afternoon, I run errands and finish up any work left over from the morning. In the evenings, my wife and I relax. We go out once or twice a week, and we make a point of having friends over at least twice a month. Life is good. We are not rich, but we are happy. *¡Mi vida en la Republica Dominicana es casi perfecta!*

I am happy to give advice to those who have read this and feel they need to know something else. I would also love to hear your stories and Dominican Republic experiences. My email address is <u>Ross@MovingtoDR.com</u>. I will respond to emails as quickly as possible. I will do my best to be open and give unbiased advice. You can use it if you want, and you can delete it if you don't want to listen. I am not getting paid for any advice, so take it for what it is worth. With that said, there are several kinds of people for whom I simply have no time. First, I will not listen to "Poor Me, Pity Me" stories. I will also not read emails from people who try to sell me stuff. I make my purchasing decisions in the same manner I made my move to the Dominican Republic: very cautiously and with a lot of research.

My Short-List of Things I LOVE:

70-*peso* movies
Fresh fruit and vegetables, particularly the avocados and
mangos
Mangú (smashed plantains with cheese and onions
–similar to mashed potatoes – man, this is good!)
Pastalon de platano maduro (sweet plantain casserole
with beef)
Rice and beans
My *Mata de plátano* (Plantain tree) that now has seven
leaves
The breeze that blows through my house all day long
The beaches
The coconuts
The laid-back lifestyle: who would ever think it would
be all right to be an hour late?
Real Dominican families: the bond Dominican families
have never ceases to amaze me.

Bonus Materials

This book is much more than the printed material you are holding. In fact, there are several other parts and many pictures I wanted to include; but due to printing and space restrictions, I was unable to do so. I have hidden a password in this book for you to be able to access this additional material on my website: www.MovingtoDR. com (See website for details on how to find them…)

Here are some examples of what you will find:
- **Things about which I know nothing** – Drugs and Prostitutes.
- **My final frustration**—getting directions from a Dominican.
- **Periodic updates** of things I continue to learn.
- **More funny stories** of experiences that either totally caught me off guard or that got the best of me.
- **Great pictures** of many of the things I write about.
- **Job and income listings** for current opportunities in the Dominican Republic.

A Few Last-Minute Extras

Additional Reading

***Four-Hour Work Week*:** About a year into my move, I read this book and was fascinated by the idea that a person could actually go on mini-vacations. In reality, I was already living that way. I was working like crazy one week, and then going off to Paradise the next. I love the mentality of this book, even though I do not quite agree with the moneymaking ability it claims. It contains some good ideas about making money while you are going on your mini-retirement. I would read them with an eye to opening your mind and to thinking in unexpected and unusual ways. This book is a great resource.

***Total Money Makeover*:** This is Dave Ramsey's book on getting out of debt. I believe that most North Americans and Europeans are burdened by too much debt. We are used to buying with a credit card now, and then paying for the item over time. This is a big problem. I wish I had read this book five years ago, so I could have been further down the path to a debt-free life. The principle that has helped me most through the transition was my emergency fund. I have saved enough money to live without any income for six months. I will actually be able to make it much longer because some of my investment properties are paying more than just part of their way. Read this book, and then put its teachings to work for your financial future.

My Top Picks for Dominican Getaways

   The Dominican Republic boasts such a broad array of activities that it's difficult for a first-timer to figure out the best way to spend those vacation hours. I would recommend that those who have never been to a resort or an all-inclusive spot spend at least a day or two at one of these amazing places. It's always fun to go to a place where you are encouraged to eat and drink all you can possibly handle without worrying about the bill.

   If you have been to an all-inclusive resort before, I would recommend doing something different. After all, how different is an all-inclusive in Cancún from one in Puerta Vallarta, Mexico? They are all the same. Once you have been to one, you know what they're all like. I vote you skip them completely and really enjoy the country by doing something out of your norm. Here are a couple of my favorite places. I haven't been everywhere, but I have been to many places, and these few are the best.

   When you are ready to take it up a notch in your travels, consider some of these vacation spots. Some will probably cost a few more dollars than that cheap all-inclusive you found on the Internet, but they are well worth the price. In my opinion, in fact, it is better to spend a little more for a really nice room and eat a little less. In the end, the quality of the resort is what matters. If you get a chance try out some of these secret spots. (They are not really secret, but they are a little different from the normal first-time visitor's hangouts). I also recommend these spots because once you move to the Dominican Republic, you will no longer find it fun to hang out where all the tourists are. Being around a bunch of loud and often drunken Americans is something I don't want to do anymore on my vacations. Get out of the touristy places, and you will really start to know what the Dominican Republic is all about.

<u>Bahía de Águilas (Bay of Eagles).</u> This area is located about a five-hour drive up the coast westward toward Haiti. On the way there, you will pass through some of the most amazing landscapes imaginable on a tropical island. There are the normal crowded little towns. There are lakes and rivers. One of the most interesting areas for me was the vast cactus desert. Yes, a desert! In the Dominican Republic! It is unbelievable. There are miles and miles of cactus plants. It looks like an area that gets no rain. I can only imagine there are times there is a lot of rain; but from the drive by, it looks as if it hasn't rained in years.

   The bay is secluded from development and is virgin territory. It's located in an ecological reserve, so there is currently no development; I hope it stays that way. There are no hotels or modern amenities. It is pretty much just you and nature. There's a very small village of shacks, built for the people who make their living from the few tourists passing through each day. Other that the small village of locals who make a living by taking people back and forth to the beach, there is no commercial business for many, many miles. In my recollection, we had not passed a gas station for probably close to two hours, which means close to four hours of driving between stops!

   When you arrive, there is only one shop/store/restaurant. If you are thirsty or hungry and didn't bring anything with you, this is the only choice you have, so enjoy it. The point of getting this far in your adventure is not to spend the day looking at the ocean. The point is to get into a small boat that will take you for a twenty-to-thirty-minute ride to the beach. You should arrange with the people in the restaurant to have a boat take you to the beach, and also a specific time for them to come and pick you up. It would not be fun to be left there overnight! The boat ride is incredibly beautiful. It goes past sharp rock cliffs. The ocean is crystal clear, and you can see the bottom seemingly only a few feet below, even though it must be many meters deep in places.

Once you are on the beach at Bahía de Águilas you will experience the most pristine beach you've ever seen in your life. There are no signs of civilization. There are no people living there, nor are there any places to buy things. To be fair, I did hear there are very rugged trails for 4x4 vehicles to take to get to the beach, but I did not see any sign of vehicles other than some old overgrown-looking trails.

Your day at the beach will be one you won't soon forget. We were not very prepared. We had purchased several umbrellas, but they were cheap and not of good quality; and by the end of the day they had all been torn to shreds by the wind. We had plenty of food and drinks, so that was great. I only wish I had brought a snorkel and fins, as the water was simply magical. The sand is some of the whitest sand I have ever seen, even in pictures. It was as if the line where the sand and water met never existed, almost impossible to determine if the water was one foot deep or ten. It was simply astonishing.

After you have had your fill of sun and sand, your boat will arrive to take you back to the store. You'll be able to purchase some wonderfully fresh fish and enjoy drinks while the rest of your group is trolleyed back from the beach. This is one of the highlights of my time in the

Dominican Republic. We spent a weekend at a very nice lodge with friends to celebrate a birthday. One of the day excursions was to the Bahía de Águilas. I would love to go back and to be a little more prepared for the day at the beach. This is by far my top pick for a must-see in the Dominican Republic.

<u>Punta Cana and Cap Cana</u>. Okay, so this one is a touristy place. Nevertheless, it is simply amazing, and I definitely recommend seeing it. Now, assuming you are not going to do the whole all-inclusive thing but would like to go to the beach, you should try the Punta Cana Resort. It is an unforgettable place. The slogan at this resort is, "Do anything you want, or nothing at all," and it's true: you can enjoy yourself either way. The resort has a breathtaking beach and an excellent swimming pool. There's a world-class golf course with at least one hole requiring you to shoot over the water. The amenities, in my opinion, rival any five-star resort in the world. The food is moderately priced and breakfast is included. In my experience, this is absolutely the best resort, and I believe the value is hard to beat.

While you are at Punta Cana you have to take the time to visit Cap Cana. The Cap Cana project is going to be the crown jewel of the island. It is slated to have the largest marina in the Caribbean. During our visit, Ana and I had the opportunity to eat at a restaurant named *La Marrana*, which means "the pig" in Spanish. This restaurant was a highlight of my vacation. Situated overlooking the harbor, *La Marrana* offers incredible service, with an attentive staff whose recommendations for appetizers and entrées were perfect choices. I rank the atmosphere of the restaurant in the top ten worldwide.

The food is easily top-tier and the staff was unbeatable. Cap Cana has done well by choosing this restaurant, as it showcases the area's continued development. (***While I have been writing this book, La Marrana has moved to Santo Domingo.)

The rest of the resort is also marvelous. There are many yachts in the harbor to look at. The beaches are extraordinarily beautiful, and the harbor is always full of yachts – a wonderful sight. I didn't have a chance to visit the hotel district, so I can't comment on that area, but several of the hotels have very good reputations. For an unforgettable experience, I highly recommend taking the time to walk around the marina and a quick stop at La Marana for a bite to eat. Of course, if you have a yacht or a boatload of money, you can do a lot more in Cap Cana than I did while I was there. If you'd like a companion, let me know.

Jarbacoa. Jarbacoa is known as "the Dominican Alps". Jarbacoa is located in the mountainous region in the middle of the country. The temperature in Jarbacoa is usually ten to fifteen degrees lower than the rest of the country; so during the summer months, when the heat and humidity elsewhere is almost unbearable, is the best time to visit. Ana and I spent the first two nights of our honeymoon at a lodge in Jarbacoa. I wouldn't recommend going to Jarbacoa in the middle of winter, because it was a little colder than I would have preferred. The lodge was very nice and sat right on the edge of a river. It was very peaceful; listening to the sound of the water rushing by was really relaxing.

We have also spent some time at Rancho Baiguate, which is marketed as "An Adventurer's Hotel". They offer many different activities, a pool, and many games to keep you busy. While we were there, we took a guided horseback ride up to the big waterfall nearby. All in all, we had a lot of fun. When my family visits from the US, they make it a point to go to Rancho Baiguate at least for a day because they are hooked on Canyoning. This is an activity that requires you to hike, rappel, ride a zip line, and swim. It is a fairly strenuous activity, so if you have any worries about your health, I would recommend checking with them before you sign up. I plan to go with them next time they visit. I've seen the pictures they took, and it looks like a great time. You can try many other adventure-related activities: for example, you can rent four-wheelers, go white-water rafting, and ride mountain bikes.

In my opinion, you don't necessarily have to make a trip to Jarbacoa on your first trip to the Dominican Republic. However, if you find yourself sick of the beaches and sun – or once you have moved here and you're looking for something a little different to do, it is a great place to go. Take your time and drive around. If you can get a friend or family member to show you some of the backcountry, it is well worth just driving around and enjoying the views, which are breathtaking.

Samana. Although I have never actually stayed overnight in Samana, the day I spent walking around the city and taking in the views made me fall in love with it almost immediately. I was also very taken by the beautiful scenery on the way driving to and from Samana. I am including Samana because there are whale-watching excursions at certain times of the year. I believe they are during the winter, when the whales are spending time in the warmer southern waters. I would recommend taking a whale-watching trip if you are in Samana.

I would rank Samana close to Punta Cana with regard to the quality of beach and the availability of activities. We visited several beaches and saw some unforgettable landscapes. Most of the country's green coconuts, which are used for coconut water, are grown in Samana. There are thousands of acres of coconut trees. Playa *Rincón* is one of the most beautiful beaches I have ever seen. Because it is not secluded there's a lot of traffic. This beach is unique in having a cold freshwater stream running into it, which has not yet been ruined by overdevelopment.

<u>Cruise Out of Santo Domingo</u>. I do not recommend the cruise out of Santo Domingo for you if you're visiting the country for the first time. Neither do I recommend the cruise if you have to fly to Santo Domingo to take it. If you have to fly here for the cruise, skip the cruise and explore the island instead. This island has so many extraordinary places, and such a wide variety of people and activities! In my air travels, I frequently meet people who fly in on Sunday morning for a cruise that leaves on Sunday night. Then they return the following Sunday, only to head to the airport for their flight home. It is such a shame to hear these people say that they have been to the Dominican Republic. I just tell them they are making a huge mistake; if they really want to experience something new, they need to stick around here for a week when they return from their trip.

However, once you've moved to the Dominican Republic, if you are ever in need of a week-long getaway, taking the Cruise out of Santo Domingo is one of the coolest ways to do it. There are great locals' fares available through many local travel agents who book the rooms at the last minute when they do not sell. I have seen week-long cruises for as low as $400. You'll see several other islands, and get a taste of how different all the islands in the Caribbean are. Some are desert islands; some are very flat; and some are really just a mountain sticking up out of the water. This cruise will show you all of them.

Resources. The learning curve is large for a person who is making the move to the DR. You are going to have to learn when to trust people and when people are trying to take advantage of you. You've probably noticed that throughout this book, I have tried to point out many situations where you need to keep your awareness sharp. I've also tried to show you how to steer clear of potential pitfalls. In the end, there is going to come a time when you will have to gut-check some things, and go with what feels right. I recommend studying and internalizing as much as you can about your new environment before you get here. I have used many different resources and have learned to trust some of them. I have also learned that some people are just out to make money from me, or worse. It has been necessary for me to learn how to prevent that from happening in the future. Here are my guidelines for how to be able to tell if something is worthwhile:

- Good: I consider a resource "good" if it is reliable. This doesn't mean it tells you what you want to hear; and it doesn't mean it tells you the same things all the time. It means that the resource gives you the same type of information, or information from the same perspective, every time. I do not have a problem with someone making money off me. Some of the most important people in my life, particularly advisors, count on the money I pay them to make their living. Remember this: people who are paid by you can still be great resources, as long as they are upfront about it. In your dealings with them, keep in the back of your mind the fact that their relationship with you is a source of income for them. For example, when you have your lawyer help you file your immigration papers, he or she will make money when you pay the fee. The fee will be known and disclosed upfront. Perfect.

- <u>BS (Bit Suspect).</u> BS resources are those that are suspect because you don't know if they are telling you the truth, or you don't know if their bias is consistent. An example of BS resources would be the guy selling me the meat at the airport who told me the meat was great. He was making money from me, and I had no way to protect myself. Usually BS resources are people you have to rely on; but they are actually unreliable, and often they see the relationship with you only as a source of money. Before I give my house keys to anyone, I always test that person to make certain he or she is trustworthy.

When someone you don't know very well offers to have "their friend" fix something for you, be careful. Such people may not really be doing you a favor. You have no guarantee that the friend does even marginally decent work; and you can be pretty sure that the person giving the referral will get a kick-back from the friend. If you are taking referrals from people who have an interest, or who may have an interest, be very wary.

Finally, in the BS category, some expatriates who live in this country feel that they have to prove something. They have lived here for years, been through good and bad times, and they have had many experiences. In many situations, they feel that their recommendations should carry as much weight as the words of the ancient prophets. They want you to look up to them as if they were Methuselah. Often these people are retired and have nothing better to do than offer well-intentioned but unsolicited advice. I think they deserve respect for their accomplishments; but they are not necessarily to be trusted, just because they speak the same language you do. Many old-timers are even worse than the locals. It is easy to test people. Give your trust a little bit at a time, slowly. If your trust is betrayed, make sure the person has to earn it back with twice the effort of the first time around.

<u>My Most Highly-Recommended Resources and How to Use Them</u> (I am not compensated by any of these places, so I have nothing to gain whether or not you use them. I also list updated resources on my website: check out <u>www.MovingtoDR.com</u>).

DR1.com. This is one of the best sites related strictly to the Dominican Republic. There are daily news updates on the home page and they have an excellent online forum. With regard to the forum, I have joined and posted a few times. The reason I don't actively participate is that there is way too much drama caused by the "old timers" for me to want to get involved. I find there are several users who provide invaluable information and advice, but there are many, many others who are simply jerks. I recommend reading and reading and reading. I can't think of any topic that is not discussed. Remember this is a public forum, so mind your manners and respect people. You will learn to love many things about this forum.

Yahoo.com. I read Yahoo news daily. It's one of the sites that help me keep current on things around the world. In addition to reading the news, I also read Yahoo's weather page, bookmarked for the Dominican Republic. I like seeing where the storms are, and find this a great way to see them from above. Sometimes I use Yahoo's finance page to see what the exchange rate is, but I have found it's always a bit higher than I actually get here.

SuperCasas.com. Looking for a house or apartment? This is a great resource for finding what's out there, and for starting to gauge prices.

SuperCarros.com. This is the sister site of *SuperCasas. com.* If you're looking for a used car, this is a great way to see what's out there. As long as you know what you are looking for, you may be able to find a good deal here.

Cine.com.do. All the movie theaters around the country

list their current movies and show times on this site. You have to know about this site so you can check the times of the movies in your area.

Dominicantoday.com. An English-language news website that will keep you up to speed on all the current happenings in the DR. It is a great resource.

Once Your Spanish Is Better

Menu.com.do. Hungry? Want something delivered? This site has restaurants, their menus, and contact information so you can get their goods delivered right to your door. The only issue here is that you have to be able to order in Spanish!

Lapulga.com.do. The real *La Pulga* is the market on the east side of Santo Domingo that opens every Sunday. Locals go there to buy cheap stuff. I have never gone there – it's a madhouse, and the stuff looks as if it came from a second-hand store. Lapulga.com.do. is the Dominican version of EBay. You can list items for sale and people will contact you if they want to buy it. The only downside is that you have to meet people in person to conduct your transactions; but this is the Dominican Republic, so it doesn't make much sense to try to mail anything.

Diariolibre.com. The top DR news site, ranked by its daily traffic.

Elnacional.com.do. The second most popular DR news site, ranked by its daily traffic.

Hoy.com.do. The third-ranked DR news site, according to its traffic.

Work-Related Resources

Monster.com. This is the world's largest job board. Positions in the Dominican Republic are often listed here. Virtual jobs, as well as jobs requiring travel, are also listed. You can search forever!

Elance.com. If you have a skill and want to use it to do work for people on a freelance basis, this is the place to advertise your service. I have used this site several times. The number of high-quality people who use it is amazing.

6figurejobs.com. As its name indicates, this site posts only higher-income jobs. It's a little tough to find such jobs located in the Dominican Republic, but jobs requiring travel are often listed.

Infoempleos.net. This is the Dominican Republic job site. Many different options are posted here, with jobs in almost every salary range.

GATavers.com. Dominican-Republic-based recruiters post positions here. If you are looking for work, make sure they have your resume.

Internet Marketing

Godaddy.com. This is the best site to register your domain names.

Vodahost.com. These folks have an unlimited hosting plan for website owners. The only restriction is the number of merchant accounts that can be hooked to shopping carts.

7Search.com. This site offers great pay-per-click search service. If you need inexpensive traffic, this is the way to go.

Commissionjunction.com. This affiliate referral site allows you to make money by placing ads from other businesses on your site.

Embassies

You should know the contact information of your country's embassy and follow their instructions for registering.

British Embassy. http://ukindominicanrepublic.fco.gov.uk/en/

Canadian Embassy. http://www.canuckabroad.com/canadian-embassy/dominican/santadomingo.shtml

US Embassy. http://santodomingo.usembassy.gov/

Spanish Vocabulary

Many of the great Dominicanisms are really contractions of "true" Spanish.

<u>Cómo tu tá?</u> = This is a must-know phrase that in real Spanish is "cómo está usted?" It means *"how are you doing?"* Use it for a salutation. It works wonders, because Dominicans will recognize you are learning Dominican Spanish.

<u>DR</u> = Abbreviation for the Dominican Republic. Dominicans never say "the Dominican". It's always "La Republica Dominicana" or "La Republica". You can abbreviate it in a sentence as DR or RD and Dominicans will understand. Do not say "the Dominican", it just sounds bad.

<u>Cedula</u> = Your Dominican Identification card. You will get it when you get your residency papers.

<u>Gineo</u> = A banana. Get used to calling it "gineo" because that's what it is.

<u>Aplatanado</u> = A term used to describe the process of a *gringo* beginning to become Dominican. The term means that you're eating enough bananas or plantains to actually change into a Dominican.

<u>Colmado</u> = This is a convenience store, like the Dominican 7-11. They have anything you need and are open most of the day. If Americans could ever get over their love of

suing people, corner stores would be able to afford to send kids on scooters to deliver things. The problem is that insurance and liability issues in the US make it impossible to have delivery for such small orders. If Americans ever tried it, they would love to have the service of a Colmado. Colmados will deliver whatever you want right to your front door. The Colmado is TERRIFIC!

Jeepeta = Literally means "little jeep". *Jeepeta* refers to all the small SUVs seen everywhere in the Dominican Republic. They range from Hondas and Toyotas to Porsches, Hummers, Range Rovers and Mercedes.

Limoncillos = A delicious fruit available in the summer and fall. The flesh is like a grape with one large seed in the middle. The skin is the texture of a citrus. It is the size of a large grape, or just smaller than a golf ball.

Mangú = A wonderful meal! Green plantains are boiled and then mashed, and usually covered with grated cheese and onions. The name supposedly comes from a *gringo* who was visiting, and ate this very popular dish. He exclaimed, "Man! Good!" so the Dominicans named it *Mangú*.

Malecón = This is the name for the road that runs along the ocean in almost every city in the Dominican Republic. In Santo Domingo, the Malecón is the main road running from the colonial district all the way to Costa Verde, about a five-mile stretch.

Mirador = The park in the capital that runs along the ridge and is parallel to the ocean. Get to know the Mirador if you are into fitness, or need a place for outdoor activities. It is a beautiful park.

Moto = Dominicans ride all sorts of motorcycles. They range from small scooters all the way up to the rare Harley Davidson. As well, many different types and styles of dirt bikes are ridden around town. The term *moto* refers to motorcycles driven by Dominicans.

Moro = This staple of the DR diet consists of rice and beans mixed while cooked.

Plátano = Plantain. A plantain is a type of large green banana, much larger than the normal American bananas. Plantains are always served cooked instead of raw.

Reggeton = Dominican-style or Latin-style rap music. It is very popular with people of all ages.

Tá bien = Another great Dominicanism. This is a contraction of *"Está bien"* in "real" Spanish. It means *"I'm fine,"* or *"Everything's okay."*

Note from the Author

As I have written, and in many cases re-written, this book, I have gone through many different phases of exactly how to present my experiences and lessons. At times I took the liberty of embellishing stories in order to assist in their readability and understanding; sometimes I mixed two people or situations into one story to make a specific point. I have tried to maintain the lessons learned and to show the true colors of my move to the Dominican Republic. If any of my stories, explanations, or narratives sounds too good to be true, remember – unbelievable things happen in the Dominican Republic every day.

ACKNOWLEDGMENTS

First and foremost, I want to thank my beautiful wife for her unwavering love and support. If it were not for her I would NEVER have come to know the DR. Also, without her suggestions and prompting, this book would never have made it this far.

Thanks also to:

Julio for his friendship and for introducing me to the Dominican Republic. He instigated something that has changed my life.

Tono and Candida for their support and help in teaching me the ways of the Dominican Republic. They both have accompanied me on many unforgettable experiences.

To my brothers Jacob and Mike for always being there to talk when I have had it with the DR.

My best friend Jon for continuing to be close, even though we now live 4000 miles apart. His friendship is one of the main things I have missed due to my move.

My mother and my Aunt Marita for reading and making comments on a very rough version of this manuscript. Each of their insights made significant impacts on the finished book.

My friend Ricardo for his ability to see humor in all that life brings. He has helped me to see things from an entirely new perspective.

My Editor, Betsy Gordon, with *PublishingGurus. com*, for helping me turn a bunch of words into a masterpiece. Her superb guidance every step of the way helped me make this book a reality.

My cover and book designer, Wicked Sunny also with *PublishingGurus.com*, for taking a rough idea of a cover and making it amazing. Without the numerous hours of feverish work from Betsy and Sunny, this book would have never been this good.

In addition to my family and friends who have either asked not to be mentioned personally (or whom I may have inadvertently left out), I want to thank all of the members of my American and Dominican families. With out the encouragement from these two ever-growing groups of supporters I would be completely lost, and to list every one of them and why I want to thank them would require another book! I have been blessed to have so many people supporting and encouraging me through each of my quests.

And last but certainly not least, to all the readers who email me (ross@MovingtoDR.com) to say how much they liked (or in some cases disliked) this book. Writing a book is not easy, but to know people read and respond makes the work worth it.

Made in the USA
Lexington, KY
26 April 2012